ALSO BY MAGGIE & NIGEL PERCY

Learn Dowsing: Your Natural Psychic Power

The Nature Of Intuition: Understand & Harness Your Intuitive Ability

Dowsing For Health: Awaken Your Hidden Talent

101 Amazing Things You Can Do With Dowsing

Dowsing Ethics: Replacing Intentions With Integrity

Dowsing: Practical Enlightenment

The Dowsing State: Secret Key To Accurate Dowsing

Ask The Right Question: The Essential Sourcebook Of Good Dowsing Questions

The Dowsing Encyclopedia

Pendulums for Guidance & Healing

Healing Made Simple: Change Your Mind & Improve Your Health

Dowsing Reference Library

Caring For Your Animal Companion

The Essence Of Dowsing by Nigel Percy

The Credibility Of Dowsing, edited by Nigel Percy

THE BUSY PERSON'S GUIDE

THE COMPLETE SERIES ON ENERGY CLEARING

MAGGIE PERCY
NIGEL PERCY

Copyright © 2021 Maggie & Nigel Percy

ISBN: 978-1-946014-43-6 (Ebook version)

ISBN: 978-1-946014-40-5 (Paperback version)

All rights reserved. No part of this publication may be reproduced, distributed or transmitted in any form or by any means, including photocopying, recording, or other electronic or mechanical methods, without the prior written permission of the publisher, except in the case of brief quotations embodied in critical reviews and certain other noncommercial uses permitted by copyright law. For permission requests, write to the publisher, addressed "Attention: Permissions Coordinator," at the address below.

Sixth Sense Books

150 Buck Run E

Dahlonega, GA 30533

Email address: discoveringdowsing@gmail.com

CONTENTS

Preface   ix

THE BUSY PERSON'S GUIDE TO ENERGY CLEARING
Busy Person's Guides, Book 1

Introduction	3
How To Use This Guide	5
1. What Is Energy Clearing?	7
2. Everything Is Energy	10
3. Definition Of Energy	11
4. Effects Of Energy	16
5. Types Of Energy	21
6. Vibrational Frequency	25
7. Energy Is Dynamic	29
8. You Are Powerful	33
9. The Role Of Intention	37
10. Permission	40
11. Goals	43
12. Focus	47
13. Making Intention Work	51
14. How To Choose A Method	54
15. Dowsing	56
16. Detachment	60
17. Getting Help	63
18. Measuring Results	66
19. Clearing Curse Energy	68
20. Space Clearing	73
21. Clearing Entities	77
22. Clearing Subconscious Beliefs	82
23. Clearing The Energetic Causes Of Health Problems	87
24. Pitfalls: Stubborn Situations	90
25. Pitfalls: Personal Challenges	94
26. Protection	96
27. Success Stories	98

28. Summary   102
29. Step-by-Step Instructions   104

THE BUSY PERSON'S GUIDE TO SPACE CLEARING
Busy Person's Guides, Book 2

Introduction   109
  How To Use This Guide   111
1. What Is Space Clearing?   113
2. Why Clear Your Space?   115
3. Symptoms Of Noxious Energy   117
4. Effects Of Noxious Energy   120
5. Types Of Noxious Energy   122
6. Not Everyone Is Affected The Same   134
7. How To Sense Noxious Energies   138
8. Dowsing Energies   141
9. Dowsing Basics   143
10. Intentions, Goals, Focus   147
11. Permission   149
12. Protection   154
13. Helpers   159
14. How Often To Clear   161
15. Space Clearing "Tools"   163
16. After The Clearing   166
17. Step-by-Step Instructions   169
18. On Site Space Clearing   174
19. Long Distance Space Clearing   178
20. Map Dowsing For Space Clearing   183
21. Pitfalls   186
22. Building Confidence   192
23. Effects Of Emotions & Beliefs   194
24. Beliefs & Vibration   197
25. Feng Shui   202
26. Success Stories   204
27. Summary   207

THE BUSY PERSON'S GUIDE TO GHOSTS, CURSES & ALIENS
Busy Person's Guides, Book 3

Introduction	211
How To Use This Guide	213

PART I
GHOSTS

1. What Are They?	217
2. Why Are They Here?	221
3. Effects Of Entities	223
4. How To Approach Entities	226
5. Protection	228
6. How To Clear Entities	231
7. How Often To Clear	233
8. "Good" Ghosts	235
9. How Dowsing Can Help	236
10. Dangers, Pitfalls & Special Cases	238
11. Summary	244

PART II
CURSES

12. What Are Curses?	247
13. Types Of Curses	249
14. Effects Of Curses	252
15. Protection	254
16. Curses & Free Will	256
17. How To Disempower Curses	259
18. The Role Of Dowsing	262
19. Special Cases & Techniques	263
20. How To Minimize Curse Effects	267
21. Summary	273

PART III
ALIENS

22. What Are Aliens?	277
23. Types Of Alien Energies	280
24. Are All Aliens Bad?	282
25. Effects Of Alien Energies	284
26. Protection	288
27. The Role Of Dowsing	291

28. How To Clear Alien Energies	293
29. Special Cases	296
30. Minimizing Alien Energies	300
31. Summary	303
How Dowsing Can Help	304
Final Summary	307
How Not To Be Overwhelmed	309
Resources	313
Please Leave a Review	315
About the Authors	317

PREFACE

In November of 2021 we made a change to our Busy Person's Guide series. Previously, there were four volumes in the series. Now, there are three.

We felt the fourth volume, *The Busy Person's Guide to Natural Health*, was a valuable addition to the series, but it didn't really align with the focus of the first three books, which covered various types of energy clearing. To create a laser focus on energy clearing, what it is, the different types and methods and how to apply them, we felt it made sense to limit the Complete Series to the first three books.

By combining all three books, we're able to give readers all of the training in one place at a discounted price. Our goal is to help you become competent quickly at doing energy clearings of all kinds. We want you to be safe and effective.

If you happen to be a dowser, we give you additional ways to improve your results by including dowsing in the process. For more on dowsing, see the Resources section at the end of the book.

The world is a magical, complex place that has many invisible aspects. The more you know about what you cannot see, the better able you will be to manifest the happy, healthy and prosperous life you desire.

Maggie Percy

November 10, 2021

THE BUSY PERSON'S GUIDE TO ENERGY CLEARING

BUSY PERSON'S GUIDES, BOOK 1

Copyright © 2017 Maggie & Nigel Percy

ISBN: 978-1-946014-23-8

All rights reserved. No part of this publication may be reproduced, distributed or transmitted in any form or by any means, including photocopying, recording, or other electronic or mechanical methods, without the prior written permission of the publisher, except in the case of brief quotations embodied in critical reviews and certain other noncommercial uses permitted by copyright law. For permission requests, write to the publisher, addressed "Attention: Permissions Coordinator," at the address below.

Sixth Sense Books

150 Buck Run E

Dahlonega, GA 30533

Email address: discoveringdowsing@gmail.com

INTRODUCTION

You're reading this book because you're interested in learning about how to clear energy using simple methods, but life keeps getting busier, and it's hard to find the time to read a bunch of books or take a course.

You just want to learn whatever you need to know so you can get started, no frills and no useless facts. But energy clearing isn't as simple as 1-2-3. There is no single method that works in all situations, so anyone who only gives you a stepwise energy clearing method has not done you a service. In this guide, we give you a concise but solid foundation in what energy is, how it can affect you, and how you can transform it, as well as the knowledge you need to act ethically and safely while you do energy clearing.

The subtle difference is the same as between 'give a man a fish' and 'teach a man to fish.' If we hand you a few step-by-step instructions for clearing energy, that would not allow you to grow into a masterful clearer of energies. By giving you a foundation in energy, protection and ethics, as well as basic clearing methods, *The Busy Person's Guide To Energy Clearing* will help you quickly become competent to do energy clearing in all kinds of situations, and it will give you tools for expanding beyond the most common energy clearing jobs listed in this guide.

We must provide a warning, however. There is no way to endow you *instantly* with what you need to know. Learning is a process. While our guide is as concise as possible, you will still have to read, digest and practice what we teach. And we encourage you to continue your education after you complete this guide.

Depending on your commitment, interest and how much time you have to devote, you can master the material in *The Busy Person's Guide To Energy Clearing* in one intense weekend or a leisurely month of study. Either way, that's a remarkable achievement for so small an investment of time and money.

If you want to learn more about energy clearing after completing this guide (and trust us, there is much more to learn), we provide suggestions for you at the end of the book.

HOW TO USE THIS GUIDE

We've created *The Busy Person's Guide To Energy Clearing* to be packed with all the information you need to become competent in energy clearing, but you still need to commit to learning the material if you want to master it.

If you can find several hours to dive into the book, you can cover it in one intensive day. We think you'll remember it better and have more fun if you spread out the learning experience over a longer time period.

Most people can complete the book by spending as little as ten minutes a day for less than a month. So break it down into as many small chunks as needed to accommodate your schedule and attention span.

Just follow these steps to get the most out of it.

Step 1: Don't skip any parts. There are no unnecessary sections. Each chapter builds on the previous one. If you're really busy, just do one section a day. Commit to doing that until you complete the book. Each section takes on average 10 minutes or less to complete.

Step 2: Do all the exercises. We suggest you get a journal or notebook to write your results in. You don't create competency by memorizing facts. You become masterful by applying what you have learned, by thinking deeply about it. Your participation is a unique aspect of these guides and helps you to learn faster.

Step 3: Get out and practice what you've learned and improve your life.

A Final Reminder:

Don't skip the exercises. Don't skip anything. The goal is not to see how quickly you can finish the guide; the goal is to master all the material in it, because only by doing that can you hope to be competent at energy clearing.

1

WHAT IS ENERGY CLEARING?

Energy clearing is a New Age-y subject with ancient roots. Usually when someone talks about clearing energy, they are referring to making changes in the invisible forces that negatively influence your mental and physical health, finances, relationships, career and business.

So-called 'modern' culture often ignores the invisible forces at work in your life unless it can measure them. For example, no one was bothered about radiation until science found ways to measure it and determine it was harmful to health, but regardless, radiation has always been detrimental. Marie Curie, Nobel Prize-winning scientist who discovered the properties of radium, died due to exposure to radiation. Too bad science at the time had no idea radiation was dangerous.

Never assume that what science says is the last word. The actuality of science is that it is always changing and ever-growing, thus, it is a mistake to act as if what science 'knows' today is the final word in anything. Whether science can measure them or not, there are energies that are harmful to your health and well-being, and it is in your best interest to learn to deal with them effectively.

Historically, most cultures acknowledged that there are invisible forces, energies, that can have positive or negative effects on your health and well-being. Some of the detrimental energies are inanimate energies, like noxious earth energies, while others have elements of consciousness, like ghosts and other discarnates, or curses.

In the past, various rituals were practiced, often by medicine men/women or priests, to neutralize the effects of detrimental energies. Exorcism and the blessing of crops, livestock and homes are examples of energy clearing techniques that have been practiced for centuries. Sage wands, incense, crystals and symbols have been used as energy clearing tools for hundreds, if not thousands, of years.

It is not necessary to have a professional perform energy clearing in many cases, but you do need to know what you are doing if you want to effectively clear energy yourself. By learning the basics and practicing them, you will not only enhance your life experience, you will save money by not having to turn to a professional.

In this guide, we are going to give you a solid foundation in energy clearing so that you can quickly begin to perform simple, effective energy clearings for yourself. Energy clearing looks very simple. And it is. But to be effective, you need to have the proper outlook and technique to get results. Anyone can wave a sage wand around. It isn't the sage wand that is doing the work, as you will find out in this guide.

Our goal is to show you the magic behind the prayers, the sage wand and the other tools professionals use in order to clear energy, to help you understand that tools are not the whole story. Much of what you will learn in this guide is a honing of natural abilities you don't use a lot. It is subtle. It is commonsensical. It is simple. But leave any of these elements out, and you won't be successful.

We're going to give you the blueprint for approaching energy clearing the way professionals do. If you take the time to learn and practice what is in this guide, you will get results. Our guide will instruct you in the skills, the mindset, the tools, the pitfalls and the most common applications for energy clearing. We also include instruction on ethics and protection, both vital topics.

As with any skill, mastery will require practice and further training, so don't stop with this guide. This guide is just the beginning, but it will allow you to get out there and see results fairly quickly. It's an incredibly affordable way to dip your toe into this vast, vital and intriguing topic.

2

EVERYTHING IS ENERGY

You may have learned in school that the Universe is composed of both energy and matter. Matter is physical stuff, like you and rivers and birds. But most of the Universe is energy, and energy is invisible for the most part. Historically in modern society, people were more concerned with physical objects, but as science developed instruments that could detect things that are invisible to the eye, energy became a bigger focus.

As it turns out, modern science doesn't really regard matter—physical stuff—as that different from energy. Matter is just another form of energy. So ultimately, *everything* is energy. Having this viewpoint is not only more accurate scientifically; it allows you to look at energy clearing with less skepticism and greater clarity.

In this guide, you will learn the basics about transforming energy. Energy transformation (or clearing) is a powerful, almost magical tool for improving your life, because it allows you to change detrimental energy to beneficial.

3

DEFINITION OF ENERGY

To learn how to clear energy, you need to know what energy is. You may have a vague idea of what energy is, but if you try to define it, you will probably get bogged down. That's because energy is a term that applies to many different things, so it's important to understand what you mean when you talk about energy.

In Wikipedia it says, "Energy is an indirectly observed property in physics which comes in many forms." Huh? What the heck does that mean?

Maybe we should find another definition! In grade school, you might have learned that energy is the ability to perform work. Does that allow you to picture what energy is? Not really.

The word' energy' can mean many things. If you are ill, you might feel you don't have 'energy'. A charismatic person might be said to have a certain 'energy.' An 'energetic' person is someone who is very active. To physicists, 'energy' can exist in a variety of forms, such as electrical, mechanical, chemical, thermal, or nuclear. By now, you can see that the word 'energy' has many definitions, and none of them seem to apply to energy clearing.

You want to know about energies that can be cleared and the methods for doing that. So the term 'energy' in this guide has a very specific meaning that does not relate to motivation, activity level or physics. In this guide, we use 'energy' to describe invisible vibrational frequencies that have an effect on you. The effect may be measurable or not. The effect may be noticeable or subtle. The effect may be beneficial or detrimental. The effect often varies in intensity from one person to another, or from one species to another.

Be warned that trying to define 'vibrational frequency' when used in this way can be nearly as confusing as defining the term 'energy.' You'll do best by trying to get a 'feel' for what energy means, rather than trying to find a usable definition.

Energy is real, but it's invisible. Energy affects you, but might not affect your sister or your cat in the same way it affects you. Energy changes. Energy is everywhere. In this guide, we'll be looking at how invisible energies that affect human beings can be detected and altered to create more positive outcomes.

Because there are many different perceptions of energy, there are many approaches to it. In this guide, we share our professional experience and perception of energy and give you tools that have worked for us over many years in lots of situations for ourselves and our clients. Your interest in this vast, varied and undefinable quantity called energy shows you are a rare and special person, and we're pretty sure that using the methods in this book will help you make positive changes in your life.

Exercise

Get a notebook, journal or folder with some blank sheets of paper so you can keep all your exercises and observations together. You may find it useful to date the exercises and to go back later and review them as you become more knowledgeable.

1. Who's your favorite friend? Think about that person. What do you wish for that person to experience? Think of something very specific that goes along with how you feel about him or her. Write it down.

What you just did was send energy to that person. Your intention that she experience success in her job or win the lottery or find a wonderful mate was positive energy flowing from you, and energy has an effect.

If the exercise had said pick a person you strongly dislike and think of something you wish them to experience, that would be an exercise in cursing someone, and we don't believe in doing that. But you can see that energy coming from a conscious source (you) can be either negative or positive for the receiver of the energy.

2. Energy can also come from sources that don't have the level of consciousness that humans have. Have you ever visited a place that felt heavenly to you? That you didn't want to leave? Where was that place? What did you tell yourself was the reason for feeling so good? Write it down.

Did you try to say you felt good there because you were on vacation or the weather was nice or you were in a fancy hotel and you didn't have to fix your own meals or clean your living space? You were just rationalizing. The physical environment is a reflection of the energy of a place. So the energy there was inherently good, and your feeling good was a sign that the energy's effect on you was beneficial.

3. Have you ever been somewhere that makes you fearful or wish to get away as fast as possible? Where was it? What were the conditions? Did you rationalize it? Write down the answers.

4. Not all places can be judged by how they look. Can you think of a place that felt bad, even though you could not rationalize why you felt scared or bad? While the environment might physically reflect detrimental energies, it does not have to. Write a description of that place and explain how it didn't seem to make sense for you to feel as you did. An example would be going somewhere familiar, but feeling very different from how you usually feel, or going somewhere that looks nice, but feeling really scared or nervous.

Things To Do

You have the ability to sense the energies of a place and their overall effect on you. This is a survival trait that you can sharpen. Try to use that sensing ability daily. Get a feel for how your basement or attic 'feels' energetically. Sense your workspace. What words best describe how each of these places feel to you? Do they change from day to day? Why do you think that is?

If you have children or pets, they are often sensitive to energies, but unable to express what they are feeling in ways you understand. A child might tell you there's a monster in the basement or something in the bathroom tried to kidnap her. A pet might avoid certain areas—one example we see is horses veering away from an area repeatedly when going around an arena or round pen, or a dog on a walk suddenly jogging to the side as if to avoid something in the same place every day. Since dogs and horses are like humans, you want to pay attention to what they avoid. Cats, on the other hand, often seek out energies that are noxious to humans, like EMFs, but knowing that will also help you see 'bad' spots in your home. Your cat sleeping on your computer keyboard is actually a sign that it isn't healthy for you to be close to it for hours at a time.

Think of several places you frequent and write down how those places make you feel. Later in the guide, you'll be given ways to change the energies so they feel good to you.

What You Learned

The exercises are building blocks for your understanding of this complex topic.

In this section, you learned that energy, though invisible, can be sensed, and your reactions and feelings often tell you whether the energy of a place is beneficial or detrimental for you. You can also learn from the reactions of children and pets. If you practice, you will find your sensations improve, deepen and give you more information.

To get the most out of these exercises, take time to really think, to reflect and to write down answers and to reflect on what you have learned.

4
EFFECTS OF ENERGY

The Invisible Root Cause Of Everything

Like X-rays or carbon monoxide, energy can't be seen or detected by your physical senses. But it's still there. And it always has an effect on you. Energy can affect you beneficially or detrimentally.

That's because we live in a dualistic world. A dualistic world like earth is made of polar opposites. Right and wrong. Good and bad. Up and down. You can never get rid of all the 'bad' stuff in a dualistic world, just like you can't get rid of all the 'up' stuff and only have 'down'.

So you'll never be able to totally rid the world of 'bad' energies, but you have to power to transform the ones affecting you to beneficial, at least for a period of time. And that can give you space to live more happily.

Energies impact your health, relationships, state of mind, finances…all aspects of your life. In fact, energies are the root cause of everything you see in physical reality. It can be hard to make changes in life, but changes are easier if you work on transforming the root cause of a condition or situation, rather than treating just symptoms.

An example would be if you get headaches a lot, you might take aspirin to get rid of the pain. And it works. But you keep getting headaches, and so you have to take aspirin regularly. That is because you are treating the effect, not the cause.

The cause is sometimes hard to find, and humans are naturally lazy, so taking a pill seems preferable to hunting down causes. But what if you find out the cause of your headaches is that you are allergic or sensitive to caffeine? Would you be willing to forego caffeine to get rid of the headaches and stop paying for aspirin? Probably. Transforming the energies causing your situation is like discovering that your headaches are caused by caffeine, and you have the power to stop them.

Remember that you can measure the effects (sometimes called 'level in effects') of energy on you (or anything else) using a scale of +10 to -10, with 0 being neutral. Since you are a busy person, your best bet is to focus on discovering energies that are -8 or worse for you and deal with them. Then, if you have more time, you can work on the lesser noxious energies. How can you tell what the level in effects of an energy are? Read on for suggestions.

Dosage Matters

Noxious energy is like poison. The effects depend on dosage. In this case, dosage means how long you are exposed to the energies or how powerful the energy is. A -8 energy is very bad for you, but if you just walk through a zone of -8 energy, you will be much less affected than if you are sleeping 8 hours a night in a zone of -8 energy. So while finding the really bad energy is important, it's even more important to assure that areas you spend a lot of time in are healthy for you. That means your bed, your desk at work, and your favorite chair you watch TV in.

Directed Energy

What if the noxious energy isn't something like environmental energy? What if it is directed at you, like a curse or alien experiment or an attached entity? The type of energy does have an impact on how noxious the effects will be. A -8 or -9 earth energy that is stationary and you can move away from is much less dangerous than a -9 curse or an entity attachment that is -8. Certain types of energy 'follow' you around or are attached to you. They will have a greater effect, and if they are highly noxious, they can be especially harmful to you.

Like Attracts Like

The law of attraction says that like attracts like. It will save you time and effort if you learn to release or transform your own anger, fear, victim and grief energies, as these will only attract more of the same to you. There are many ways of accomplishing this goal. Meditation and many harmonizing techniques like the art of Jin Shin Jyutsu are effective. By working to harmonize yourself daily, you will find you need to clear less often, because you won't be as likely to attract noxious or inharmonious energies.

How Can You Tell?

You can tell whether there are detrimental energies effecting you by looking at the state of your health and well-being. If you have ill health, poor mental function, a lot of fears, relationship and financial problems, then you probably have significant detrimental energy affecting you.

If you want to know details about the kind of energy, you need to develop the ability to sense and differentiate between them. As to the level in effects of the energies, they usually correlate well with how challenging your circumstances are. The more disharmonious and soaked in detrimental energies you are, the more effects you will feel, or at least you will have stronger effects from stronger noxious energies.

Exercise

The severity of your symptoms/challenges reflect the energy affecting you. (We won't worry now about 'where' the energy is, or what type it is. That comes later.) Think about the most challenging situation you are facing at this time in your life. Write down the symptoms and describe the situation. It can be something about health, a relationship or your finances. What outcome do you want instead? What have you done to try and change it? How hard has it seemed to change this situation? How long has it been affecting you? How stressful is it?

After you have written down your answers, put aside your pen and relax. Empty your mind. Breathe deeply and slowly, in and out. Focus on the breaths. When you feel calm and your mind is still, focus on the symptom you want to change. See a scale going from -10 at the left, along a line through 0 to +10 on the right end of the line. The numbers go from -10 to -9 to -8, and so on.

Start at -10 and slowly move along the line as you tune into your problem. What number stands out as representing the strongest energy affecting your situation? For some people, a number will just pop into your head without using this scale visualization. Don't doubt your answer, however it comes to you. Write that number down. Your intuitive senses are capable of quantifying how you feel to this extent.

Usually the strongest noxious energy affecting a major issue will be a large negative number. Certainly -5 or worse; often it is -8 or worse. Whatever you got, that is the first energy you want to transform when you are working to resolve your problem. Don't doubt your feelings. Go with what you got.

Remember that there are many energies, and you might have multiple energies affecting you. So you may not be able to get instant relief by clearing a single energy. But every energy you clear helps.

What You Learned

This exercise will help you begin to exercise your natural ability to sense energies. In a later section, you will learn how to focus your intuition for better results, if you wish.

5

TYPES OF ENERGY

There are so many different kinds of energy, that putting them into categories helps you think and talk about them in more useful ways. There are two ways you can categorize energy: based on the source of the energy, or based on the effects of the energy on a species.

∼

Energies By Source

Knowing the source of the energy can be useful for helping you determine ways to transform it or mitigate its effects. If you know someone is cursing you, for example, you might deal with that energy in a different way than you would deal with geopathic energy (noxious earth energy).

You can create whatever categories you want regarding sources of energy. We have found it useful to use the following:

- Earth or geopathic energies

- Human or manmade energies
- Cosmic energies
- Other

Earth energies originate in the earth and include the effects of fault lines, radon gas, negative lines of energy that run above or below the surface of the earth and underground water, among other things. What they have in common is they originate from the earth and have a noxious effect on you and are associated with a particular geographic location.

Human energies include anything originating from people. Depending on how you define that, you might include curses, discarnates (human ghosts), EMFs (electromagnetic fields) and the normal everyday stress energy that piles up in an environment, among other things.

Cosmic energies originate outside the earth. They can come from other dimensions, other planets, from elsewhere in the cosmos. They include nonterrestrial entities, star energies, portals and alien energies, to name some of the most common.

"Other" is a category we include to make sure we don't miss anything. Some energies straddle categories, and if you find something that falls into this category, it will probably have elements of two or more of the above categories.

The above examples are not all-inclusive. There are many types of energies in each category.

It is worth mentioning that some of the above energies are more 'conscious' than others. When an energy that is affecting you originates from a conscious being, it is usually more powerful and often harder to clear and sometimes even dangerous to work with. We will be talking about this in detail later. For now, just be aware that you will handle conscious energies slightly differently.

Energies By Effect

You can also categorize energies by their effect on a certain species. In most cases, people are concerned with effects on humans, but sometimes you will want to know the effects on animals, plants or even relationships and finances. Just know that they are not always the same.

Energy affects you on a scale that goes from very detrimental (causing death), through neutral (no effect), to beneficial (helping you). We find it useful to use a number scale of +10 to -10 for this purpose. When we use it, anything -8 or worse is very noxious, and anything +8 or better is highly beneficial.

Knowing the 'level in effects' of an energy helps you decide how serious it is and how important it is for you to transform it quickly and effectively.

Using Both Types Of Categories Is Best

We use both of the above ways to characterize energies, because each gives you valuable information. Knowing both the source of the energy and its effect on you will make you more effective in your work.

How Do You Know?

How do you determine what types of energy are present and what effects they have on you? If the energy is EMFs, you can buy a device that will test them. You can research online what the effects of those energies are. For all the others, rational or scientific methods have not been created at this time to help you. So you will need to use your intuition. That is covered in a later section. If you don't have the ability or wish to determine types of energy or their effects, you can still clear energies, but it's more of a crap shoot. Kind of like baiting a hook with whatever comes to hand and wondering what type of fish you will catch…or not.

WHAT YOU LEARNED

This section will help you think about energies more clearly and give you ways to talk about them and approach clearing them, by showing you ways of categorizing energies.

6

VIBRATIONAL FREQUENCY

The concept of frequency is useful when working with energy. Everything has a vibrational frequency, and when you clear or transform energy, you are changing that frequency. It's like when you tune your radio from the jazz station to the Top 40 station, you get a big change in music. A change in frequency changes the whole tone of your life experience.

You are energy, even though you are also physical form, matter. Remember that matter is just a 'denser' form of energy. Your energy frequency affects everything you experience. The frequencies of energies in your environment are a reflection of your energy and also have an effect on you.

Your thoughts and feelings have an energetic frequency. When you are feeling angry or thinking fearful thoughts, you have one kind of frequency. When you are happy and thinking positive thoughts, you have a totally different frequency. Cultivating a truly positive and joyful attitude (and frequency) is the key to good health and well-being. But it isn't all that easy.

It has become so much the rage in the New Age movement to 'be positive' that many folks act positive, believing this is the same as actually being positive. Acting a certain way is acting, not reality. You may fool other people, and if you try hard, you may convince yourself, but you can't change your frequency by pretending.

Honesty and self-awareness, and a willingness not to judge yourself for being human (and imperfect) are major factors in altering your frequency to improve your life. If you can admit to anger, fear and other 'negative' emotions and thoughts, you can begin to change them.

Life is about the journey. On this journey, you will learn to identify and transform energy frequencies within yourself and in your environment, and you will see measurable change for the better in your life.

EXERCISE

What frequency are you currently resonating with? That will determine your life experience.

Are you able to be totally honest with yourself? Everyone is going to say 'yes' to this question at first, without even thinking. Don't do that. We spend a lot of time hiding our true emotions for many reasons: we're ashamed of them, we don't know how to express them constructively, we feel no one will validate or understand them, we feel powerless to change them.

Here are some examples of vibrational frequency 'stuffing':

- You have no idea how you're going to pay the bills next month, so you try to avoid thinking about it, because you know worrying is 'negative' and won't help.
- Your spouse is consistently unable to nurture you, and that makes you feel unimportant and unloved. You are angry about that, but since you know you can't change your spouse, you stuff your anger, because anger is 'bad.'
- At work, you have a boss or coworker who is jealous and lies about you and even tries to undermine your ability to do your job. You'd like to smack the guy in the face, but violence is

unacceptable in the workplace, and you were brought up to feel it is 'wrong' to be that angry. Also, you know that because of the system, no matter what you do to try and get a remedy, you're the one who will look like the bad guy, so you don't report the sexual harassment or lies, you just swallow your anger at the injustice.

If you have anything in your life that is cause for sadness, anger or worry, you are almost certainly vibrating with at those frequencies, even if you have stuffed your emotions.

How can you tell if you are doing this, since it can become a lifelong habit? Answer these questions: Do you judge yourself if you are angry, depressed or irritated? Do you let perfectionism become a block that guarantees you are imperfect? Do you find yourself saying, "It's all good," even when it isn't? If you say yes to even one question, you are stuffing your emotions. And those emotions are still broadcasting, whether you want them to or not.

Don't use the realization that you are stuffing emotions as another way to judge or bludgeon yourself. Finding out that you have this habit is actually a step in the right direction. Now you can do something to change your frequency.

1. Think carefully about how you are feeling about one major area in your life at this time: finances, career, health or relationships. Overall use a scale of +10 to -10 to rank your honest, deepest feelings, with 0 meaning you feel neutral. Be honest. Write it down.

What is the biggest feeling you are experiencing about this situation? Would you characterize that feeling as positive, negative or neutral in frequency? Why?

Do you feel like something outside of you must change in order for you to feel better overall? Do you realize if that is true, you are giving your power away to another person or situation over which you have no control, and that locks in the current state of affairs?

Do you feel capable of improving your frequency to be one of greater happiness or at least less negativity? What are some things you could do to resonate more with the frequency you want? Could you spend more time focusing on things that cultivate that feeling? Can you eliminate or distance yourself from troublesome subjects, people and situations? Can you go in search of solutions instead of focusing on the problem?

2. Now pick another area in your life where you really want to see improvement. This time, make it one that is 'smaller' in scope than the previous exercise, but go through all the same steps and answer the questions.

We recommend that you begin working on smaller issues that you don't feel completely powerless about and work up to the bigger ones. Each success will add to your level of confidence, to the belief that you can change your energy. In the following sections in this guide, you will get tools you need for making the changes you wish to make to your vibrational frequency.

What You Learned

Notice how this exercise shows that you have control over what you feel and how you react to things, even if you weren't aware of that. The solution to transforming your energy may not always be easy, but setting your intention is the most important step. Then follow through using methods covered in later sections.

You are a powerful being. You can resonate with whatever frequency you choose. This guide will help you do that.

7

ENERGY IS DYNAMIC

Energy is like the weather, constantly changing. Sometimes the energy is beautiful and harmonious and supportive of your goals, like a perfect summer day. Other times, it's like a tornado or a dust storm, creating irritation and negativity, even danger. It's a common misconception to think the way the energy is now is the way it will always be. Because energy is constantly changing, you need to monitor it and tweak it as needed to support your health and well-being, much as you need to tweak your diet and exercise program for optimal health.

Weather changes a lot (unless you live in the tropics, and even then you can have sun or storm, even hurricanes and typhoons), but it seems to have a predicable range of types. You learn what to expect of the weather wherever you live. But energy can appear in new forms, and it's important that you be open to seeing new and different energies in addition to the common ones you've come to expect.

Do not react in fear or feel a loss of control because of these facts. Fear is counterproductive. If you complete this book, you will have a good basic tool kit for dealing with most common energies. Knowledge is power; it should not frighten you.

This guide claims to be about energy clearing, but in fact, it is more about energy *transformation*. Energy clearing is a commonly used phrase, but energy transformation is more powerful and comprehensive. Energy clearing is parallel to doing housework. You dust, you vacuum. The dirt is collected or moved around. It is not transformed; it is just removed from your environment temporarily, and then new dirt piles up. What if your vacuum magically transformed dust and dirt into something positive? Then cleaning would become transformation. Think of how much better that would be! You don't want to just clear out bad energy. You want to create positive, supportive energy for your goals.

In this book, you will learn how to transform detrimental energy to beneficial. That is far more useful and powerful than simply removing bad energy. You can take a bad situation and turn it totally to your advantage, to help you reach your goals.

Energy cannot be permanently turned into beneficial by just one clearing. Because it is constantly changing, you need to monitor energies regularly and deal with them. Just as you clean your house regularly so it looks its best, you need to clear energies regularly for optimal well-being. Plan on monitoring your energies on a regular basis for best results.

You can do that in a variety of ways. You can observe what's going on around you, as that is an accurate reflection of energies. You can tune in intuitively and get a 'feel' for the energies. This takes a bit of practice, but is a skill anyone can learn. Lastly, the skill of dowsing is the best way to find out detailed information about the energies around you (more about that in a later section). Whatever you choose, the important thing is to monitor the energies on a regular basis.

Certain energies are challenging to resolve. You transform them, and they come back. Among those types are active curses, which are powered by the ill wishes of another human being. The curses that are pointed at you are the most stubborn. It is possible to 'pick up' curse energy not aimed at you due to some resonance within you, and that is more easily cleared in one session.

Another type that can be challenging is entities. If they do not want to move on, they often 'run away' when they see you intend to do a clearing. Then, they return after you are done. But the majority of energy will respond to a single clearing/transformation.

EXERCISE

The easiest way to find out about energies that are affecting you is to observe what's going on around you and how you feel. You have nonphysical senses that are meant to help guide you in your pursuit of health and well-being. You may be adept at using them, or you may be like most people, unaware that you have them, and thus, a bit clumsy at first when tuning in. Regardless of your level of experience using your nonphysical senses, you can become quite good if you practice.

In your notebook, describe the most prevalent patterns you are seeing in your life at this time over the past month or two by answering these questions:

First, make a list: physical health, mental/emotional health, relationships, finances, career. In each category, answer the following questions: How are you **feeling** compared to the past about this part of your life? Happier? More stressed? Ungrounded? Successful? Frustrated? How would you quantify your emotions on a 0-10 scale, with 8 or larger being very intense?

What new patterns are you seeing in terms of money, health and relationships? Are they improvements or not? Try to describe them in a few concise words and phrases.

What old patterns seem to linger, no matter what you do to try and change them?

What would you like to be experiencing and feeling at this time instead of what you are experiencing?

If you had to rate your situation overall on a scale of +10 to -10, with 0 being neutral and positive numbers meaning success and happiness, what number would you give overall to your current situation? Do this for each category.

You will notice that in areas of your life that are most stressful and farthest from what you want to experience, the negative numbers are higher.

That number is probably a good indicator of the severity of detrimental energies in your life at this time. If the number is -8 or worse, you definitely need to do some work. And this guide will show you how.

8

YOU ARE POWERFUL

All human beings are capable of transforming energies from detrimental to beneficial. You have the power to sense and change energies within you and outside of you. You have natural senses to support the process of energy detection and transformation. They are intuitive senses rather than physical senses.

Physical senses relate to physical matter. Intuitive senses relate to nonphysical things like energies. Your feelings are your compass to help guide you as you sense your way along the path of life. Good feelings are feedback that you are on the path; bad feelings let you know you are somehow out of alignment.

In talking about good and bad feelings, we don't want you to be confused by the false good feelings escapism can create within you. Humans turn to drugs, alcohol, sex and other behaviors to escape the stress of everyday living. Escaping feels better to some people than facing life's challenges. Such escapism can lead to unhealthy addictions that are a substitute for actually feeling good about life. When you are feeling good due to escapist behavior, you know it, because you are avoiding life and what is stressing you. When you feel good actually living your life, that is a deeper emotion and a sign that you are in alignment with your life's purpose and goals. Don't beat yourself up for wanting to escape sometimes. We all feel that way. But do try to avoid patterns of avoiding life through escapist behavior. They are diversions that end up wasting time and often have negative side effects.

Though it sounds simple to pay attention to your feelings, it is not always easy. Humans tend to be ruled by their emotions rather than using them as a guidance system.

You are naturally a powerful being, but through extensive programming and trauma, you probably have lost sight of that fact. You might even equate power with evil, using examples of corrupt government and corporate officials as what you do not want to be. Power does not equal evil. Power is neutral and can be used for either good or evil. You get to choose. Your life will be much better if you can accept your natural power to choose and then go about exercising it however you feel is best.

Powerless people do not resonate with being able to transform energy from detrimental to beneficial, so it is vital that you stop seeing yourself as powerless.

Exercise

You've heard people say, "It's all good," and that sounds like how you ought to feel. But unless you truly mean it, it's the same thing as saying, "I don't care."

It can be really tough to feel good when things are going wrong. And just saying it's good does not make it good. In fact, it is a sign that you are judging your feelings as bad, and you want to change them, so you are hiding from them.

Remember that bad feelings are necessary and a vital part of your guidance system. No feeling is 'wrong.' No feeling should be eliminated. Acknowledging your feelings is the first step to improving your life situation.

Example: many people get trapped in depression because they judge anger as bad. They've been taught it's wrong to be angry, so they bury it. When they push it down, they end up feeling powerless and depressed, which are actually heavier frequencies. If anger breaks through, they push it back down, returning to powerlessness, and it becomes a vicious cycle. Anger is actually a 'higher' frequency than depression. You just do not want to dwell in anger. But it's ok to be angry, especially if you use it to make choices to change your life.

1. What feelings do you judge are negative and try to avoid feeling them? Write them down.

How would your life change if you used those feelings as a sign and tried to change your situation for the better? Are you afraid if you face those feelings, you will have to make changes you can't imagine, like getting a different job, avoiding certain friends and family members or even divorcing your spouse? Face them anyway. You can choose whether to take action or not, but it is a huge positive step to acknowledge how you feel.

If you feel trapped in a situation, and that's why you bury your negative emotions, what are some things you can do to relieve the stress or move in the direction of a solution?

Examples:

If you have a bad health problem, have you researched therapies for resolving it? Have you tried new diets, alternative therapies, things to help you feel empowered to make change? Try something and see.

If you feel trapped in a difficult relationship, like a bad marriage, or you are caring for an aging parent, do you give yourself permission to take time for your own mental health? You can always make time for 15-30 minutes of 'me' time. Meditate, read a fun book, soak in the tub, go for a walk. Get away from stress for a while and go out in Nature and think of lovely things. The key is to do something that uplifts you. It won't magically change everything, but if you do it regularly, it will reduce stress and lead to improved health.

Feel stuck in poverty mode? Instead of getting a third job or taking out a second mortgage, why not look into improving your own sense of worth and value? If you resonate with worth-less-ness, you will be poor.

There are many simple ways to improve your self-esteem. EFT (Emotional Freedom Technique) is easy to learn. Affirmations work for some people, but can be problematic. Vision boards are useful for visual folks. Journaling and making goals can help align you with positive change by changing your focus and refining your intentions.

What You Learned

Recognizing that you are powerful because you control how you react to things or feel about them, and that you can tell what is good for you and what isn't by how you feel, is an amazing awareness that empowers you to begin to make changes and create the life you want. But you may find that you have to work to change your attitudes, beliefs and normal reactions if you want to see real progress. Don't feel bad. That's normal. It gets easier if you keep doing it.

9

THE ROLE OF INTENTION

How do you use this power you have to transform energies? The key ingredient is intention.

Intention refers to an aim or plan you have. You may think you already have an obvious intention. You want to clear energies. But *why* do you want to do that? Your intention involves knowing what particular outcome you are trying to attain by that clearing.

Is your intention to improve your health? Your relationships? Your finances? To help your dog or cat? To protect your children? To create a harmonious place to live? To have a more productive garden? To finally finish writing that novel?

Your intention is what powers your process. It is the basis for the success of every clearing and healing modality. Without intention, you don't generally get results. If you have no intention, it's like mouthing a prayer without thinking why you are saying it. Lip service doesn't give results. Intention does.

Intention alone, though, does not accomplish much. It's kind of like wishing for something. Dreaming and wishing are nice, but rarely end up giving us what we want. They can be a type of escapist behavior unless they are linked to active choosing.

You need to combine will with intention to get results. Will power is the power of choosing. We live in a free will Universe. We have the right to choose. When you choose to experience what you intend, that is an unbeatable combination.

The exercise of choice can be a challenge. If you are resonating with powerlessness, you won't feel you have a choice. In fact, if you are in a bad situation and you find yourself thinking you have *no* choice, you are eliminating a key element that is needed to change things. You need to have a dream of what you intend to experience, but you also must choose to experience it and commit to doing whatever it takes.

When you choose to take action that you believe will help you reach your goals, that is putting intention to work for you. It is surprising how few people actually do this.

∾

Exercise

Get your notebook and write down one intention you have for yourself. What would you like to experience that you are not experiencing now?

How do you feel when you write that intention down? Do you have negative feelings, like doubt or powerlessness? Your reaction will tell you how much you are in alignment with that intention, how close in frequency you are to expressing it.

What choices could you make that would show you are exercising your will power, your freedom to choose a certain outcome? Break them down into small steps that feel doable to you if you can. Then try to apply them.

∾

WHAT YOU LEARNED

Having an intention and choosing to follow through on it are vital components to success. Don't let negative self-talk sabotage you as you take this first step to becoming powerful at transforming energy and improving your life.

10

PERMISSION

Be Ethical

It is perfectly ethical for you to clear energy for yourself and your children and pets. But for anyone else, including other family members, you need verbal permission.

The reason you need permission is that clearing energy is an invasive process and you need to respect the privacy and beliefs of other people. Not everyone is open to the idea of energy clearing. You have the right to your beliefs; others have the right to theirs. It is inappropriate to override others' beliefs with your own, no matter how good you think they are.

Even when working with children and pets, check if they are willing to let you help. Most of the time, they are, but sometimes, they are not. If you work on anyone without permission, you won't get permanent results, as this is a free will Universe. And you will be creating negative karma for yourself by ignoring their boundaries. People who mess with other people's energy often find that their boundaries are not respected by others. Show others the respect you want. **You'd want someone to ask you before trying to change your energy to fit their beliefs.**

Dowsing may be used to determine if a very small child or pet is willing to accept your help, since they cannot talk, but for older children and adults, you must obtain their verbal permission. In a later section, we explain basic dowsing. To work on someone else's pet, at least ask for permission from the owner before doing a clearing.

∽

Exercise

Ethics is a very personal thing. You need to be able to think critically. What are your values? What do you believe? Can you argue that your choice is an ethical one, and would others accept your argument?

Let's look at an example. You have a good friend who is addicted to cigarettes. You find smoking an obnoxious habit and you also fear for your friend's health if she keeps doing it. Is it ethical for you to do a clearing on her for whatever is causing her addiction without her verbal permission?

How would you argue in favor of doing the clearing? Would you base it on your judgment that smoking is bad, therefore you have a right to stamp it out? That you have good intentions, so anything you do is appropriate, even if she didn't ask?

You need to think critically. Clearly, your friend has chosen to smoke. Even if she knows it isn't healthy, she is doing it. She might say she can't help it, that it's an addiction. But if she has not approached you about helping her change, you have no right to decide she must change to suit your values or beliefs.

Talk to your friend. If she says she'd like your help, then it is ethical to do so. If you are afraid to talk with her, you have your answer. You know she isn't open to what you want to do. So don't do it.

∽

What You Learned

Respect that this is a free will Universe, and many, many people do not act as you would like. That does not give you the right to try and change them using energy clearing and other powerful techniques without their permission. Such behavior on your part is a sign of fear and shows disrespect of free will. Anything that overrides or denies free will in another person without their consent is not ethical.

The ethical exercise of power is not discussed often, but it should be. In our guides, we are empowering you to do things that can radically improve your life, but those powers can be abused, just like any power. It is vital that you handle this power in an ethical and sensitive way.

11

GOALS

In order to create a particular outcome, you want to create an energetic atmosphere that supports that goal. In order to do that, you need a clear vision of what your goal is.

The goal is the end result you wish to create that is an expression of your intention, which becomes manifest as you make choices and take actions that you believe will help you reach that goal.

Before you clear energies, take the time to identify your intention. In your mind, have a clear goal that you want to reach as a result of the energy work you do. It can be helpful to write this goal down in your notebook, so you can come back later and see how the results match your plan. It takes practice to create really specific goals, and by reviewing the process after the fact, you can refine your technique and boost your learning curve.

Various experts say there are 5 or 6 elements to a good goal. One system says a good goal is SMART: specific, measurable, achievable, realistic and timely.

It is vital that your goal be 'specific' and 'measurable', or you won't know if you succeeded.

As to 'realistic' and 'achievable', that relates to your beliefs. Many successful people ignore what the masses say is 'realistic' and go on to achieving great things, as in breaking the sound barrier or running a 4-minute mile. The important thing is *you* need to believe your goal is achievable, even if no one else does.

'Timely' relates to having a time frame in mind for reaching your goal. You want to set a realistic time frame you can believe in. If you accept what everyone says, that is how it will work for you. Great inventors believe in their ability to create something amazing that challenges current thinking. You can do just about anything if you firmly believe in it.

Let's look at a fuzzy goal and how you would make it SMART.

Say you are 10 pounds heavier than you want to be and your clothes don't fit and you hate looking at your naked body in the mirror. You are thinking of doing energy clearing or transformation to help you change.

What is your intention? What is your goal?

If you just want to lose weight, that is kind of a negative goal, plus it is not really a goal. It is a process you are committing to. But why lose weight? What do you want to achieve?

Really, you probably want to look good in your clothes, to feel fit and trim, to be able to look at yourself in the mirror and think well of how you look. These are goals.

You think losing weight will achieve those goals for you, but it is only one path. Certainly losing weight is specific and measurable, and you can set a time limit for it. It is an achievable and realistic goal.

But if that is your only goal, you will then make choices you believe will help, such as changes in your diet.

Yet you know most diets fail, and you could end up here again. In fact, you have probably been here before. So maybe your goal needs to be broader than just losing ten pounds. Maybe the energetic cause of your problem isn't your weight. It's how you feel about your body.

If you decide you want to feel better about your body, you might choose another set of actions. You might decide to do some EFT to help you love yourself more and quit judging yourself. You might decide to clear false beliefs about beauty equalling a thin body. Perhaps you will find it useful to work with a therapist about past traumas that caused you to judge yourself as unworthy or ugly because of something someone else did to you. Maybe dieting isn't even the answer. Perhaps if you change how you feel and think about yourself, you will naturally lose weight.

So be sure to set goals that represent what you *really* want to experience.

EXERCISE

Think of something you want to change in your life. What would you like to experience instead? You can use the subject from the last section if you like. Write it down.

What would your goal be? Use the SMART system and be very specific about what exactly you want to experience. Don't make the mistake of making the *process* your goal, as in losing weight. What is the actual thing you want to experience that will change your situation?

Is that goal specific? Is it measurable? How would you measure it? Write it down.

What time frame would you give yourself for this process? Do you feel the goal is achievable and realistic and doable in that time period? If not, write down why not.

If you aren't totally on board with your goal, you won't be able to focus your intention. You will sabotage yourself.

This exercise makes you think in detail about goals, and that will help you set better goals that will be more achievable.

WHAT YOU LEARNED

Energy clearing can be used for many goals. Some of the most common are: having a healthy and harmonious space to live and work, manifesting what you want and being fit and healthy. It is surprising how many people can tell you what they don't want to experience, but they have trouble expressing what they do want to experience, and that is a block to their success. By being able to clearly state your goals, you will find it easier to discover and clear energies that are blocking you.

12

FOCUS

To become a wizard at energy clearing, you need to have focus. In fantasies, the wizard is powerful because he has a magic wand or knows arcane words. That's what they want you to think. It is misdirection. The most powerful tool of a magician is focus.

Energy clearing is like magic. You transform something detrimental into something beneficial. That makes you a magician. But don't get caught up in wondering whether it's OK to wear metal or which direction you should face while doing a clearing.

It is a common misunderstanding in the New Age community that the power is in the tool or the ritual itself. Know this: the power is within you, and if you have clear goals and are able to focus your intention, you will be successful. Rituals are only a crutch to help you focus. Yes, we all need training wheels when learning to ride a bike, but don't get trapped in rituals once you have gained confidence, and don't give them power.

"Focus" is about being able to pay particular attention to something. If you have specific goals, but you lack focus, your clearing probably won't work. In fact, that's probably why so few people can get intention to work for them. So then they opt for fancy tools and words and rituals, but they still aren't focused, so they still don't get results.

Multitasking is the enemy of focus. You must do one thing at a time if you want to become proficient at energy clearing. Trying to do more than one thing leads to mistakes and actually takes longer.

Another enemy of focus is emotions, if you allow them to control you. It is human and natural to experience fear or worry or elation, but if you want to learn how to clear energies, you must be able to put aside your emotions and work with detachment, which we will talk more about later. This doesn't mean you are a robot; it means you work with a clear mind.

A little-known but common reason that intention doesn't work is that most people don't have the energy level to power their intention. Weakened energy fields are common in 85% of the people we have tested, so strengthening your energy field is helpful for improving your results. It's a whole course in itself to train you about your body's bioelectromagnetic field. For the purposes of this book, certain common sense behaviors will improve your field's strength. Avoid toxic foods, situations, emotions and people. Organic food, pure water, happy thoughts and pleasant, supportive people strengthen you. So don't watch the news or sit around bitching with your friends. Do things that make you feel good. If you feel trapped in a life of doing mostly what feels bad, you need to make some big changes. Get help if you aren't up to the task yourself. A strong energy field makes you better at focusing your intention, so it's worth doing whatever it takes.

How can you tell if you are focused? Do stray thoughts jump into your head while you are trying to focus? Do you lose the train of thought? Do you start thinking ahead about some future event? Focus means being able to hold one clear thought in your mind for as long as it takes to get the job done.

The Abraham-Hicks method says that if you focus on one thing for over 17 seconds, it must come to you. Sounds easy, doesn't it? Try it sometime. It's not that easy. In order to clear energy, you need that kind of focus.

You can increase your ability to focus by forcing yourself to only do one thing at a time, all the time.

Another good behavior is to slow down. Rushing around might give you the perception that you are accomplishing a lot, but slowing down and doing one thing at a time the best you can will actually accomplish more.

Another way to improve focus is to learn how to be comfortable doing nothing. Meditating works. Or just sitting in your garden under a tree, not thinking or reading or doing anything. If you can empty your mind for a period of time, you can apply that discipline to focusing on whatever you wish to clear or change.

Another way to improve focus is to practice dowsing, an intuitive method covered in a later chapter. Accurate dowsing requires you to be able to focus, and dowsing regularly enhances that ability.

Exercise

See how challenging focus is for you by doing this exercise. Find a quiet room with a comfortable chair. Make sure you are hydrated and have emptied your bladder to avoid distractions. Get a stopwatch to measure how long you can focus.

Sit down and measure how long you are able to focus on one thought without any distractions derailing you. Pick one of the following, one which resonates with you, or make up your own. Visualize only thoughts relevant to that particular subject. The minute you start wandering off on a tangent, mark how long you lasted.

- I am connected to Source and feel Source energy flow abundantly through me.

- Picture a loved one and an experience you'd like them to have, a good experience, and visualize it happening for them.

- Focus on the color blue. Just that. See the color. Feel the color. Be the color.

- Picture a perfect flower. Focus on that flower. Allow yourself to immerse yourself in that flower.

How long did you last? Do a couple different examples and see if some are easier than others. Do you find it easy to visualize? If so, you are lucky. But if not, do not despair. You can improve your ability by practicing.

What You Learned

Being able to focus your intention is a requirement for successfully clearing energy, and to be focused, you need to act in ways that are not always considered valuable in modern society. You need to slow down, do one thing at a time and be detached about results. Because these behaviors are the opposite of what many people think they should do, you may need to work at becoming focused enough to clear energy effectively.

Focus will improve with practice. At first, you will need a quiet space to work, but eventually, you will be able to focus even in an environment that is very noisy and distracting. Since you plan to do energy clearing in the 'real' world, which is often chaotic, this ability will be vital to your success.

13

MAKING INTENTION WORK

If intention is so powerful, why doesn't it seem to work well when used all by itself? Prayer is actually a form of intention, when you have a clear goal of what you want to accomplish. Do you always get results when you pray? Most people don't. The same is true when using intention to clear or transform energies. Even having a specific intention and goals and choosing to take right action do not guarantee success.

Over the thousands of years of human existence, people have observed that intention works best when 'anchored' in something physical. That can be a ritual, an object, special words or anything in the physical realm. Incense at a religious rite, special words and phrases or signs and symbols used during the process, rituals that help focus one's intention, talismans and other ritual objects to wear or carry, sacrifices. All of these anchor intention. They remind the person to focus on their intention and also give an element of belief that helps the person have an optimistic outlook. Focus and belief are powerful elements in manifesting results.

Human beings for the most part are not adept at using intention by itself to achieve results. This is why prayers and statements of intention are not the most popular means of energy transformation. They work, but their success rate is not as high as methods that anchor intention.

All healing methods work by harnessing the power of intention. All energy transformation methods work via intention. Intention is the common denominator. The anchors vary and have no particular magic in and of themselves. People are drawn to rituals and objects that resonate with their energies and beliefs.

Because this is true, we'll be showing you a variety of ways that are simple and inexpensive, yet effective for anchoring your intention when clearing and transforming energies.

There is no one right way to anchor intention. There is just the right way for you. The most important thing to remember, though, is that the anchor has no magic or power in itself. It is simply a reminder to you of your goals, your focus and your attitude.

EXERCISE

The anchor you choose should be a reflection of your own energy and beliefs, so that it will be more effective. Here is an incomplete list of possible anchors:

- Symbols
- Colors
- Fragrance
- Words/statements
- Ritual
- Object, such as crystals
- Sound

Do any of the above draw your eye? The ones you are most attracted to are probably your best starting point.

In your notebook, write down which anchors attract you the most. Think about why that might be. Is it because of something in your history, your education, your culture? Or is it something inexplicable? Speculate as to why those methods are magnetic to you. Why might they resonate with the power to change things for you?

There are no right or wrong answers. The idea is to gain insight into the resonant energy, so that you can capitalize on that.

Anchors can be simple or complex. Remember, they don't work better because they are complicated. They don't work better because they cost a lot. Simple, free anchors can work every bit as well as complex, expensive anchors. The only requirement is that the anchor resonate with your energy.

By resonate, we mean that you believe that you will be more effective by using that anchor. Your belief may be a reflection of your religious upbringing, your culture or even past life influences. When you pick an anchor that feels powerful to you, you enhance your chance of success.

Most anchors can be things you buy for very little money or make yourself. Which anchor you choose will depend on what you are trying to clear, your own energy and other factors.

You won't use exactly the same anchor every time you clear energies. You may use crystals all the time, but you won't use the same one over and over. You may prefer symbols, but you will find it necessary to change them.

You match the energy of the anchor with the energy of the project and your current energy. So while you may choose colors as your favorite form of anchor, you will vary the color and how you apply it, depending on the energy you are clearing.

It may frustrate you to hear that we can't give you a short list of anchors that are guaranteed to work for you. But the fact is that you, the situation you are working in, and the anchor must all match up for success, and there are millions of combinations to choose from. Don't worry! Your intuition will guide you in this process once you have your goals formulated.

14

HOW TO CHOOSE A METHOD

Choosing a good anchor for clearing energy is as simple as tuning in to your goals and then being drawn to the best answer. Your intuition is powerful and will guide you in choices like this. If you practice, you will find it easier to tap into your natural intuitive ability.

You will want to have an extensive list of things you are open to using. In addition to those mentioned before, you might add a variety of other possibilities, like numbers or flowers. Anything can be an anchor, and you will benefit by staying open to using whatever will work best for you in a given situation.

∽

Exercise

The anchor you choose depends on the job and your own energy. There is no wrong answer. Get your notebook and do this exercise and write down any observations you have afterwards.

You want to clear some detrimental energy that is affecting your workspace. Every time you sit at your desk, you feel it. It makes you irritable and unfocused. You feel unproductive.

So you decide to do a clearing. Your goal is something like, "I want to be surrounded at work with energy that supports productivity, creativity, accuracy and enjoyment of my work environment." (If you do not work, then pick a location you frequent in your home instead.)

You then focus on that goal, on the place you are clearing, and you look at a list of possible anchors. Here is a possible list:

- Color
- Symbol
- Number
- Sound
- Fragrance
- Statement of intention
- Crystal

You decide in advance that you won't use fragrance out of respect for coworkers who might have allergies. Now focus on the remaining items in the list and your goal, and let yourself be drawn to one as the best way to clear the energy in question.

What did you get? Write that choice down.

When you were drawn to that choice, did you 'see' anything more? For example, if you chose color, did you see a particular color? Or if you got crystals, did you just 'know' what crystal you wanted to use? Please write down the answer.

If you didn't get anything else, focus on it now. Knowing your goal, focus on the type of anchor you chose and ask to be shown the best option. If you get an answer, write it down. If you don't, do not worry. In the next chapter, we're going to explain a technique for focusing your intuition and getting answers.

15

DOWSING

Everyone has intuitive hits. You receive information intuitively at times, that is, not through the rational thought process.

As a society, we are trained for years in using our rational minds to get answers logically and through analysis. Yet we spend not one minute learning how to use our intuitive ability. That may explain why so few people trust their intuition or even believe they have intuition.

Any ability requires training and practice to master. Your intuition is no exception. Even if you are highly intuitive, if you never use your intuition, you won't be tremendously accurate. It's like muscles. Do they get big and strong by themselves? No. They get big and strong from using them.

How does one train intuition? There are many ways. But most of them do not overcome the biggest drawback to intuition: that it comes unbidden. You could wait around a long time and never get an intuitive hit that you want.

That is why dowsing is such a great technique. Though most people only know dowsing as a way to find water, dowsing is in fact a way to get answers to questions your mind cannot answer. Dowsing is focused intuition. Intuition on tap.

The power of dowsing is that you can use it to answer any question your mind can't answer. So when you want to choose an anchor for clearing energy, dowsing is a perfect technique to use, either to pick a method or to confirm your 'intuition.'

This guide is not a dowsing course. We have another guide on developing your intuition and a link to our dowsing course in the Resources section. We urge you to get that guide at least, because your intuition is a valuable resource. Don't let it sit unused, like a Ferrari in your garage covered by a tarp.

Learning to dowse is very straightforward, but like any skill, dowsing has complexities, and you will get better results if you get good training. What follows is just a taste of what is involved in dowsing, so you can decide if you want to plunge in and learn how to do it. Without dowsing, you are working blind in energy clearing. We strongly urge you to learn how to dowse.

Dowsing involves several steps:

1. Be clear about your goal
2. Form a good question that is very detailed and specific and has a yes or no answer
3. Focus on the question and empty your mind (this is called getting into a dowsing state)
4. Be curious but not attached as to what the answer is
5. Receive the answer

Steps 1-4 seem pretty easy to understand, though I must warn you that each one involves work and practice to master. Make a mistake at any step, and your answer will probably be incorrect.

Step 5, the actual answer, is just a small part of the process, but it may be the part which is most unfamiliar to you. When you dowse, you can either use a tool like a pendulum, or you can dowse without a tool, using some part of your body to give you the answer (the latter is what kinesiologists do).

There are many methods of deviceless dowsing, but one of the most common and most reliable is the Body Sway. The Body Sway uses the forward or backward motion of your body to indicate 'yes' or 'no.'

Give it a try. Stand straight, relaxed, feet shoulder width apart. Close your eyes. Breathe normally. Think of the city or country you were born in. Ask, "Was I born in _____?" (Fill in the blank with the correct answer.) Wait in a curious and detached way to see what your body does. Forward is usually 'yes.' Did you get forward motion?

Don't be upset if you did not. Maybe your 'yes' is backward motion. Check out your 'no' answer by doing it again, but this time, insert an answer you know is wrong for your birthplace. As long as you get a different motion for 'yes' and 'no,' you can dowse and get an answer.

How accurate your answer will be depends on how good and clear your question is, how detached and focused you are and a number of other factors we won't go into here, but are covered in the guide on intuition.

The purpose of this demonstration was to show you that it is possible to tap into your intuition in a focused way and get an answer to a question right now. We used your birthplace, because it's easy and you know what is right and wrong. When you actually dowse in the real world, you won't know if your answer is right or wrong, which is why we urge you to get our guide on developing your intuition.

Scales are used in dowsing to go beyond yes/no answers and find out the level of intensity of a noxious energy. There are many kinds of scales, but 0-10 and +10 to -10 are most common. Finding out a number value consists of asking what the intensity is and either saying each number until you get 'yes,' using a chart that shows the numbers, or just thinking the numbers in your head and going through them as a list until you get a 'yes.'

Exercise

Go back to the previous section and use the Body Sway to choose the best anchor for doing the energy clearing you wanted to do. Look at the 5 steps of dowsing and take your time. Write down what you did at each step. Write your goal down. Write down your question. Describe how you felt during steps 3 and 4. What answer did you get?

Does that answer confirm what you intuitively felt? If not, do you feel comfortable with the answer you got? Does it make sense? Does it feel right to you? Either way, this exercise shows you that dowsing has huge potential, and that being able to dowse accurately is a powerful tool for doing energy clearing.

You can also use dowsing to determine what energies are affecting you, how strong they are and to confirm they are cleared after you do your clearing.

16

DETACHMENT

What is detachment, and why do you have to practice it? In our culture, you are programmed to think that desire for a certain outcome is a measure of how successful you will be, as well as an estimate of how dedicated you are to creating a positive outcome. Thus, the more attached you are to a certain outcome, the more you are perceived as a dedicated individual who should create success.

In reality, that is not how things work. Yes, you do need to have a clear goal that is something you desire. But to effect a proper energy clearing, you need to let go of the desire to control outcomes. You have to learn detachment.

Detachment does **not** mean you don't care what happens. Detachment means you put aside emotional attachment to a particular outcome and just trust that the best outcome will happen. You know what you want. You know how you intend to create that outcome. You take right action and assume whatever happens will be positive overall.

Detachment can be challenging, especially if you like to control things, because it asks you to let go and assume things will turn out fine. How can you be expected to be detached, when you've often seen things turn out badly in life?

The Law Of Attraction says that what you focus on is what you attract. The energy you vibrate with is the energy you will get more of. Attachment to outcomes is usually accompanied by fear. The more attached, the more fearful you are. Vibrating with fear and worry about negative outcomes will cause them to be more likely.

Exercise

Think of an incident in your life that was very worrying, one for which you could not control the outcome. Maybe it was worry about the results of a medical test. Or waiting to see if you got into the college you wanted. Or hoping someone would agree to marry you.

Think of that situation. On a scale of 0-10, with 10 being the most intense, how much worry, fear or anxiety did you have about the outcome? Choose a situation that gives you 8 or higher. 10 is better.

Why was that number so high? What were you afraid would happen if the outcome was not what you wanted? Write that down.

Looking back on that incident, how would you say it turned out? Did you get a positive result or a negative one in the long run?

If you could have set aside the worry about outcomes, would it have made your life more peaceful? Are you convinced that worry helped?

On a scale of 0-10, with 10 being the most, what level of trust do you have in God/the Universe/the Higher Power that whatever happens will be for the best?

On a scale of 0-10, how strongly do you feel a need to keep tabs on every step of every process? Do you feel like without your guidance, everything will go wrong?

The higher the number for each of those two answers is, the harder detachment will be for you.

Learning detachment is learning to let go of control and trust in something greater than yourself during the energy clearing. Ego will have you concerned about doing a clearing 'right,' getting the results you want as if it's a test, or worrying about how others will react. It isn't all about you. It's about sensing the energies, choosing to transform them and doing your best. You are on a journey, and you will learn as you go. You will not always get the outcome you want, and sometimes you will make mistakes, but as long as you learn, all will be well. Detachment will help you put ego aside and learn to trust in something greater than yourself. It is also vital to your safety when working with entities.

17

GETTING HELP

Energy clearing can be hard and dangerous to your health. Some energies are easy to deal with, while others are stubborn and very harmful. Fortunately, there is help available.

Spiritual helpers abound in many forms. You may have a guardian angel you enjoy working with. Or a spirit guide. Or perhaps you prefer to connect with the energy of your totem animal. When working in Nature, the nature spirits and fairies can sometimes be helpful.

The supply of helpers is limited only by your own belief system. The only warning is that you need to be very clear about whose help you are asking when you ask for help doing energy clearing and similar work. When you ask for help, it is given. But if you are not clear about the circumstances, you can end up with more than you bargained for.

You do not want to work with beings who do not have your health and well-being at heart. You want to avoid working with beings who will not respect your free will.

Fairy tales you were told as a child have a lesson. When the hero indiscriminately asked for help and got it, sometimes he ended up turned into an animal or enslaved for years to work for whoever helped him.

You have the right to ask for help from beings who value your health and well-being and who will respect your free will. So don't send out requests to the ether, because you don't know who will respond. You may want to meditate regularly for a while to become familiar with your guardian angel, your spirit guide or maybe even an ancestor who is willing to help you.

A helper can be asked to provide additional protection for you during the energy clearing. Or you can ask the helper to enhance your intuition and ability to perform a good clearing. Your spiritual helpers can be a bridge between you in the physical realm and the energy you wish to clear, which is not in the physical realm.

Exercise

In your notebook, write down what spiritual helpers, if any, you turn to when you are in need.

Have they ever communicated with you? If so, how? How did you know it was them?

Automatic writing and dowsing are two ways you can get information about your helpers. You can find out your helper's name and other interesting details. It takes trust, but practicing trust will help you improve your detachment. Give it a try and see what information you can get from your helper(s).

If you don't have any helpers, would you like to have them? Try to meditate and connect with the type of helper you want to work with.

No one is completely alone in this life. You may not yet have connected with or identified your spiritual helpers, but you have them. If for some reason you are unable to identify them now, don't worry. Call on your angels or guides to help you, being clear about defining terms, and check in from time to time and see if they are ready to reveal themselves to you.

18

MEASURING RESULTS

One of the biggest challenges you will face when you begin this work is doubting that the energy clearing you did worked. It is perfectly normal to have these doubts, because you are used to a rational approach, and this is a very intuitive one. The best way to overcome these doubts is to be able to measure change after a clearing. That sounds reasonable, but can be hard to accomplish, because you need to think outside the box to find metrics that will work.

Being able to confirm results is vital so that you can improve. No one starts out perfect. You will learn as you go, and if you have ways to measure success, and you take the time to do so, you will be able to get better and better.

Some people don't want to be bothered with this. They do energy clearing and assume it worked. You will in a way have to do the same. You need to trust that you are competent and that what you intend will happen. But, if you never measure results, that is ego, that is fear of being shown to be imperfect. You should want to know if you succeeded, so that you can learn from your experiences and get better.

Since energy is invisible, how can you measure success?

If you are an accurate dowser, you can dowse to see if the energy has cleared. You must be masterful, though. If all you want is a rubber stamp, that's what you will get.

Another way is to see if the symptoms which you suspected were related to the energy go away. It can sometimes take a few days for all the energy to clear, but in most cases, it's rapid. When a symptom goes away and stays away, that is a pretty good sign of success.

Sometimes a symptom reduces, but doesn't go away. You can measure the degree of change by using a 0-10 scale for whatever you are measuring. You can assign a number from 0-10 that represents how strongly affected you feel or how bad the symptom is. Then, after the clearing, tune in and reevaluate. If the symptom was caused even partly by the energy, the number should reduce.

Energetically sensitive people can 'feel' a shift in the energy. If you are not naturally aware of energies, you can train yourself to be. Slow down. Do one thing at a time. Spend some time doing nothing now and then. Relax and tune in to a place or thing and sense the energies. When we do space clearings on people's homes, they usually feel a shift in the energy. They might characterize it as feeling lighter or brighter. Or they tell stories of how a neighbor asked if they'd repainted. Things just feel better, and your brain will rationalize why in its own way.

Never fear making a mistake. If you are open to it, you can learn a lot through experiences that many would call 'mistakes.' No one starts out masterful. Be kind to yourself and expect it to take time and practice to master energy clearing. But visualize yourself becoming more masterful each time you work. Energy clearing isn't a one-time deal, so just commit to improving as you go along. You can always do a second clearing as needed. Your best is always good enough.

19

CLEARING CURSE ENERGY

A curse is essentially an ill wish, a ball of negative energy that has been hurled your way, or that you picked up due to resonance with its energy, and it has a detrimental effect on you.

Types Of Curses

A curse can be categorized by when it originated. You can have a curse affecting you that originated in present time, like your brother-in-law cursed you for breaking his lawn mower the day you borrowed it.

A curse can be from some time in the past, meaning before you were even born. Perhaps someone cursed the property you now live on.

Lastly, it is possible for curses from other lifetimes to affect you, though it is more rare than the other types.

Curses can be categorized by whether they are currently being fed energy. An active curse might be your ex-boyfriend sending you negative thoughts every day, because he feels you were wrong to break up with him. The curse is fed each day, and that makes it hard to get rid of, because if you clear it, he'll just put it back on you. Most people who are doing this have no idea that what they are doing is a curse.

A curse that is not active is not being fed energy on an ongoing basis, and it is much easier to permanently clear.

You could also categorize a curse by its target. A person, place, organization or object can be cursed.

Modes Of Effect

You can be affected by a curse that someone points at you personally. But you can also be harmed by a curse that someone pointed at your home or property or business. You can also pick up curse energy that wasn't even pointed at you, because you resonate with the energy and just picked the curse energy up from someone else.

In general, those pointed directly at you are more powerful in their effect.

Symptoms

A curse can affect you physically, emotionally, financially or any other way. Unless you know someone cursed you, dowsing or some other way of focusing intuition is the only way to discover a curse is affecting you, which is why we are so keen on dowsing.

Use dowsing to find out if your symptoms are caused in part or wholly by a curse. If so, you can dowse to find out when it originated and whether it is pointed at you or at something like your home or business. You can also dowse what the intensity of the effects on you are, using a 0-10 scale. Remember that dowsing is not 100% accurate, so it isn't wise to dowse who the originator of the curse is unless you are willing not to judge that person or act on what you discover.

What If You Don't Dowse?

If you aren't a dowser, you can't be sure that you have any curse energy affecting you, but you can apply Step 2 in the clearing instructions below in a general way with the intention of clearing any curse energy that is currently affecting you.

Clearing Curses

Most curses are fairly easy to disempower using a statement of intention. A statement of intention is like a prayer and is the simplest type of clearing method. There are no magic words to use. Anything that clearly states your intention can work. An example would be: "Please transform the energy of this curse completely and transform any resonance to it that I currently have in my system." See *Can Curses Come Back* (below) for more on resonance.

Things To Avoid

Don't send curse energy back at the person who sent it. Some practitioners recommend a mirror or similar visualization that will bounce the detrimental energy back to the sender, but how does that make you any better than that person? It's hard not to be angry when someone curses you, but try anyway. In addition to creating karma for you, your anger can be used in some cases to cause you harm, because the rare curses put on you by someone who knows how are often booby-trapped to use your own anger against you.

Avoid getting into revenge mode. If you use dowsing and think you know who sent the curse, there is still a chance of error, so practice forgiveness and move on.

Measuring Results

You can measure results by seeing if the symptoms improve. In rare cases, there may be a dramatic shift. Usually, results are more subtle, and dowsing is the most accurate way to tell if you were successful in the clearing.

Can Curses Come Back?

If you find the curse returned, there is some resonant energy allowing it to affect you, and it is possible the originator is targeting you in an ongoing way. This situation is less common, and you would be well advised to get professional help if you feel this is the case, as it takes a bit of digging to find out what the 'magnets' are that are attracting or allowing the curse to affect you, and sometimes it's easier for someone else to discover them. Once you reveal what the 'magnet' is, you can clear it using basic clearing methods, and that should allow you to disempower the curse permanently. It is not ethical to take action against another person who may be cursing you; it is far better to make yourself bulletproof.

Step-by-Step Curse Clearing

1. Dowse: Is this symptom (clearly state what it is) partially or fully, directly or indirectly, caused by a curse? Note that without dowsing, you would need to consult a psychic to find out this information. If you don't dowse, go to step 2.

2. Use a statement of intention to disempower the curse that is causing the symptom. "Please clear the energy of this curse completely and transform any resonance currently in my system" is a good statement. Most simple curses will be disempowered this way. If you skipped step

1, you can alter the wording to "Please disempower any curse energy that is currently causing or affecting _____(state the symptom) and transform any resonance currently in my system." (Even if you are not being affected by a curse, it won't hurt you to do this.)

3. By observation of the symptom or by dowsing, see if the curse has been fully disempowered. If you feel it has not, you can use dowsing to delve deeper into what type of curse it is, so that you can take further action. Please note that if the curse was only part of the problem, you may need to do other clearing. Dowsing can help you determine what to do in complex situations.

20

SPACE CLEARING

Energies in your environment have a profound effect on your health, relationships and finances. If you run a storefront business, the energies in your store will affect your bottom line in many ways. Keeping the energies in your environment harmonious will improve the quality of your life and that of your whole family and all of your pets. This section is an introduction to space clearing, a topic that we have written a whole book on and a service we offered for years to our global clientele.

∽

What is Noxious Energy?

Remember that energy is judged to be positive or negative based on how it affects you, but energy is just energy, and it doesn't always have the same effect on all species or individuals.

In general, energy that is bad for you is also bad for dogs. But lots of energy that is detrimental to you is beneficial to cats.

You can use this knowledge to evaluate areas and the overall health of your space. If a cat hangs out somewhere, it might be because the energy is beneficial to him but not you. For example, cats seem to like computers and power supplies and sources of EMF. They also seem to offset the effects of some cosmic energies that are harmful to humans, which protects the humans.

If your dog is having a lot of health problems that you cannot explain, it is possible that she is taking on the energies in your home and protecting you from them. We have seen dogs die from using their natural protective instincts this way.

How Can You Tell?

Noxious energy is everywhere. It seems to be worse in highly populated areas and locations where unpleasant activities occur or have occurred in the past. Cemeteries, prisons and hospitals are particularly bad, but the places you spend the most time in are the ones that most affect you.

The energy in your bed is critical for your health, because you spend 1/3 of your life there. Any place you spend a great deal of time deserves your attention to create healthy space.

If you have symptoms that go away when you go on vacation, you probably have noxious energy at home. If you feel uncomfortable at home and restless, it may be a subconscious awareness of noxious energies. If you feel a sense of being watched or heaviness, you are probably noticing environmental energies. Trust your feelings. If you feel quite calm and peaceful, your space is probably clear.

Dowsing is the only way, other than having certain psychic abilities, that you can identify noxious energies in your environment and their effect on you. Our guide to intuition will help you if you want to develop your dowsing talent.

If you are already a dowser, you can ask a dowsing question like "What is the current level in effects on me overall of the energies in my bed/home/workspace on a scale of +10 to -10, where negative numbers indicate detrimental energy, 0 is neutral and positive numbers indicate positive energy effects." If you get a negative number, especially if it is -8 or worse, a clearing should be done.

If you can't dowse, use your intuitive ability to tune in to how a particular space 'feels' to you and assign it a number on the same scale.

STEP-BY-STEP SPACE CLEARING

Intention is what powers a space clearing. You set your mind to create safe, healthy and harmonious space to live or work. You can make a statement that includes all the factors important to you and anchor it. There is no one perfect statement. Start with something basic and modify it as needed.

1. Identify the level overall of noxious energy at the location by either dowsing or tuning in to it or just reflecting on how it feels to you and what symptoms you may have recently been experiencing.
2. Use a statement of intention to transform the energies to beneficial. A possible starting point is something like this: "Please transform the energy in my home to beneficial for all who live there, the humans and pets and all who visit. Please send all misplaced beings to their right and perfect place in the right and perfect way. Disempower any curse energies affecting the home or residents and place protection around the property to prevent noxious energies from entering the property from any source."
3. You can use any 'anchor' you wish in conjunction with the statement of intention to power it more strongly. Choose an anchor based on dowsing or your intuition as to what will help you most.
4. Evaluate results. Observe symptoms, how the place feels and dowse the overall energy effects on you if you know how to dowse. It should be positive, or at least neutral after clearing.
5. If you feel the results were not complete, re-do the statement of

intention using a different anchor. Allow the energies to settle for up to 72 hours, as sometimes they take a while to shift completely.

How Often Do You Have To Clear?

It depends totally on the location and its use. A busy, hectic or stressed-out place will need frequent clearing. You will need to clear more often if you are going through a major health challenge or divorce. A quiet place with few residents and little stress will not need as frequent clearing.

Energies change, and in the past 15+ years, we have observed that places which only needed quarterly clearing in 2005 needed monthly clearing by 2012. The general rule, though, is a high traffic or high stress situation needs more frequent clearing.

Do You Ever Need Outside Help?

On occasion, you might not be able to clear everything that is detrimental. Do not despair. Sometimes you are being protected from an energy that would be harmful to you if you actually got tangled up in it. Get a professional's advice if you feel like you are missing something important.

This book is not a complete guide to space clearing. We recommend you get our Busy Person's Guide To Space Clearing for comprehensive information on this topic.

21

CLEARING ENTITIES

We use the term 'entity' to refer to any nonphysical but conscious being. Human discarnates, called ghosts, are a type of entity. But there are other types. Some are beings who have never had physical bodies. Some come from earth; some come from other planets and dimensions. Many of these have no relationship or kinship with human form. Some are so different from humans that they can't perceive you and in some cases don't even sense you, or sense you as something like a bad smell.

Don't worry about where the entities originated. In general, entities are misplaced beings with no agenda regarding you. They are lost, confused, angry, sad and just want to go home or where they belong. You will be using intention to help them get there.

How & Why Can Entities Affect You?

All energy works on the basis of resonant frequencies. Entities can attach to you or affect you, and they are likely to do this when your energy matches theirs. If you are angry, depressed, confused, lost, in transition, fearful or irritated, and you enter a place like a shopping mall or hospital where there are entities having the same vibrational frequency, they may attach to you.

Entity attachment is usually mild in its effects, such as merely exacerbating what you already are feeling or experiencing. Or it might be more unusual. You might feel negative emotions you can't explain or physical cravings or pain you would rather not have. There is a full range of effects, and at the extreme end is that your behavior could cause you to be diagnosed as insane. Suicidal ideation is also sometimes the effect of an attached entity, and suicide sometimes (but certainly not always) is a result of the entity's effect on the person.

How Do You Know?

You're going to get tired of hearing us say that you should learn dowsing, but dowsing is the only sure way of knowing if you have an entity attached. If you can't dowse, use mental and physical changes to determine the likelihood of entity attachment.

It is more common to 'pick up' entities when you are out and about, shopping or working, than it is to encounter them at home, though that can happen, too. You can also pick up entities from other people. When you meet someone and your resonant frequency is more like that of the misplaced being attached to them, it will often jump from the other person to you.

The following symptoms can be due to entity attachment, but also might be from other causes:

- Bad behavior in children or pets
- Sudden shift to negative emotions for no good reason
- Sudden physical symptom with no obvious cause
- A sense of being watched or not alone
- Nightmares, especially in children

Non-attached Entities

Entities often are just 'floating' around in the environment; in fact, non-attached entities are more common and also less troublesome. If their energy doesn't resonate with yours, they won't attach to you and thus have less effect. But if you often clear energy, you can attract entities, because some of them realize that you have the power to send them to their right and perfect place. It's as if, as an energy worker, you have a neon sign that says, "Come here to get cleared." We have seen new healers and energy workers get overwhelmed at the demand of large numbers of entities for their services.

We urge you *not* to see yourself as responsible for sending entities to their home. If you encounter some when doing a clearing, or you 'notice' an entity at a convenient time (for Maggie, at night, strange house sounds often represent an entity wanting to go to its home), by all means use the technique below to release it from the earth plane. However, do *not* feel that simply because you *can* do this, you must do it, or that it is your mission. No matter how many hours a day you spend sending entities to their right and perfect place, there will always be more. By sending out your intention to only clear on your own terms, it is like turning off the neon sign, and you won't be swamped anymore.

Step-by-Step Clearing Technique

1. Determine if you have entities attached. Dowsing is the best method. You can indirectly use symptoms and assume that possibly you have attachments, and just follow through with the clearing regimen. No harm will be done if you assume you need to clear entities, even if you have none.
2. Symptoms of entity attachment include feeling negative emotions far more strongly than is warranted for your current situation or having a physical symptom appear out of nowhere.

Entities floating in the environment sometimes manifest as unusual noises, smells (we had a client once who had the smell of cigarette smoke in her bathroom, but no one in her family smoked; we cleared the entity, and the smell went away) or shadowy figures that disappear when you look directly at them.

3. Use a statement of intention to release them and return them to their proper place. An example is "Please send any entities that are attached to me or in my environment to their right and perfect place in the right and perfect way." **Note we don't send them to the 'Light' or anywhere specific**, because we don't know where they belong. Not all belong or will go to the Light, whatever that is. An anchor is not usually required. Sometimes entities will 'run away' to avoid being cleared, so you can include a phrase like 'any entities that have been attached to me or have been affecting me in the past 48 hours' to be sure to include these situations.
4. Use dowsing or an observation of your symptoms to see if the clearing worked. If you feel it didn't, repeat the statement of intention again. Do so calmly and with confidence.

Is It Always Safe To Clear Entities?

The short answer is no. Getting involved with some entities is dangerous for a number of reasons. But making a statement of intention will usually be safe. On very rare occasions, if there is a dangerous entity attached to someone whom you are trying to help, you risk the entity attaching to you if your energy is more of a match. You also are at risk if you dive deeper into what the entity is and try to address it or confront it. It is *always* a mistake to act like entities are demonic or have a negative agenda or to judge or attack them. You must keep a neutral and compassionate attitude if you want to stay safe. With entities, your detachment is vital to your safety.

Can They Come Back?

If you have properly cleared an entity, it has gone to its right and perfect place and wouldn't want to come back even if it could. However, you can fail to clear an entity for a number of reasons, and in that situation, it may hang around. That will require you to do another clearing.

Can You Prevent Entity Attachment?

The best prevention is to cultivate a genuine sense of harmony and peace. You will not attract entities if you have a very different frequency from them. Most people these days are angry, frustrated and fearful. Get rid of those emotions and radiate calm and peace, and entities won't find you attractive energetically. The same is true of your home and workspace. This requires more work than it sounds like, but it is worth it. Some techniques to help would be meditation and guided visualization or self-hypnosis aimed at creating peace within you.

22

CLEARING SUBCONSCIOUS BELIEFS

You think you know what you believe. Not true. You know what you *consciously* believe. You don't know what you *subconsciously* believe, and the subconscious runs your life most of the time.

Why does this matter? For everyone, the subconscious is a minefield of faulty and negative beliefs that block you from experiencing good health, happy relationships, success and abundance. So clearing those beliefs, which in most cases are not only faulty, but totally contradict what you consciously believe and want to experience, is a vital step in improving your life.

Where do these faulty beliefs come from? Trauma and programming in this life, experiences in past lives, even inherited ancestral patterns. The field of epigenetics is rapidly revealing how powerful the environment is in shaping what we believe, experience and express by altering our genes, and how those changes affect our life experience and are even passed down through generations.

You have the power to clear faulty beliefs, but the tricky bit is finding out what they are, because the definition of subconscious beliefs is **things**

you believe that you are not aware you believe. So how do you discover them? Or do you have to in order to clear them?

Usually, you do need to become aware of a subconscious belief in order to fully clear it. That awareness is an 'aha' moment that allows you to release it.

∼

What's With The Subconscious?

Your subconscious is tasked with keeping you alive. Not happy. Not healthy. Not rich. Alive is all it cares. And many subconscious beliefs are based on traumas in this life and past lives that relate to outcomes where you either died or someone you cared about died because of something, and your subconscious made a note never to let that happen again. If you died as a result of a revolution, where the poor rose up and killed you, a wealthy landowner, at the time of death, you maybe thought, "If I hadn't been wealthy, I wouldn't have died." Thus the belief about wealth being unsafe is born, and your subconscious will steer you away from it at all costs.

∼

How To Uncover Subconscious Beliefs

There are basically two ways to discover these insidious causes of problems. The easiest way is dowsing, because dowsing allows you to ask questions about topics that your rational mind, your conscious mind, cannot answer. If you are a dowser, it's simply a matter of asking if your subconscious believes this or that. A 'yes' answer would mean you need to clear that belief.

The second, and harder, way of revealing subconscious beliefs, is to observe your life experience, the world around you and to deduce from that what it says about your subconscious beliefs, because your subconscious is creating most of your life experience.

This isn't a book training you about manifestation and the Law Of Attraction, but learning about those things will help you get a perspective on this subject that will allow you to drop judgment and feel empowered to create a better life for yourself. In the meantime, think about something major that you'd like to change in your life.

If you are currently experiencing something you don't want to experience, you can summarize it in one statement. Here are some examples:

- No one ever treats me with respect
- I can't ever save more than $100; every time I save money, an unexpected expense wipes my savings out
- I'm always getting colds and illnesses; I'm sickly
- I'm fat and ugly

Now, formulate a sentence that expresses clearly what the opposite of that experience is, in other words, what you want to experience instead. Here are examples for the above three statements:

- I want/am able to be treated respectfully by others
- I want/am able to have plenty of money (meaning an abundance, more than you need)
- I want/am able to experience excellent health
- I want/am able to express beauty through my body

Most people have trouble wording the statement of what they *do* want to experience. This is a sign of that subconscious block. Your mind is far more comfortable and able to express the negative statement of what is, rather than a clear positive statement of what you want.

If you are a dowser, you can verify the beliefs by asking, "Do I subconsciously_____" from the above list of positive statements, or your own positive statement. If you get a 'no' answer, then although you consciously want to experience that, you will not, because your subconscious isn't on board, and it's in charge.

If you aren't a dowser, do not despair. Whatever you are now experiencing is a reflection of your subconscious beliefs, so even if you cannot dowse, you know that at the subconscious level, you have issues with experiencing the positive statement in some form for some reason. While dowsing will help you clarify the statement of the belief and even help you figure out where it came from, in many cases, that is not necessary for a good clearing.

Clearing Faulty Beliefs

While some beliefs might be hard to discover, most of the ones blocking you are pretty easy to find. You just need to set aside your judgment, because lots of them won't make sense. Just laugh at them and clear them. As with all energy clearing, your intention is what matters most.

A simple statement of intention will usually clear any given belief. The statement can be something like, "Please transform the energy of this subconscious belief quickly, easily, comfortably and safely." If you are a dowser, you can then check to see if your subconscious still believes the faulty belief. If not, it's clear. If so, repeat the clearing statement and try again. If you are not a dowser, you will have to wait and see if the outward world changes for you to verify the belief is cleared.

If you can't get it to clear, then there is probably another belief behind that one, propping it up, a belief that is more foundational. Beliefs relating to safety are an example of this. Maybe you can temporarily clear the belief "I don't want to be rich," but if you have another belief that says "It's not safe for me to be rich," the original belief will reestablish itself. This is because safety is the number one priority of your subconscious.

The most common faulty beliefs begin with the following phrases:

- I don't want to
- I am not able to
- It is not safe for me to

- I have not chosen to
- It is wrong for me to
- I will die if I

You can use dowsing to see if your subconscious feels it is safe for you to experience good health, a happy marriage, trust, respect, success in your career or wealth. You can test for the safety of just about anything and then clear when you find faulty beliefs. Without dowsing, you can only assume that safety might be an issue and go ahead and clear anyway. You can see why we recommend dowsing, as it is the best way to unlock the secrets of your subconscious. But even without dowsing, you can get a lot of clearing done.

23

CLEARING THE ENERGETIC CAUSES OF HEALTH PROBLEMS

Energy clearing is one of many powerful techniques for improving your health. It would be remiss to leave health out of this guide, even though it isn't intended to be a comprehensive training on that subject.

Experts who understand the subtle energy body, the invisible aspect of the human form, agree that dis-ease is a disharmony that originates in the energy body, which, left untreated, eventually can manifest as symptoms and disease in the physical form. This outlook is opposite to that of conventional medicine, which regards disease as purely physical.

Energy is all around you and constantly interacting with you. Previous sections have given you instructions for clearing environmental energies, entities and subconscious beliefs, all of which have the ability to negatively impact your physical and mental health. While there are many mechanisms that lead to disharmony and ill health, the ones in this guide are a good first step to creating the health you desire.

We recommend that you set up a regular program for creating harmonious and healthy environmental energy to live and work in, rather than waiting for a problem to appear. Monthly clearing should work well for most residences. Workplaces usually require more frequent clearing due to higher traffic and stress. Committing to regular space clearing will help you and your family and pets stay healthier.

If you don't clear your space regularly, then you will definitely want to dowse or tune in and find out if environmental energies are the cause of any new symptoms you experience. If you get a 'yes,' then do a space clearing. But it is always better to clear regularly.

Entity Clearing & Health

Entities are not usually a big cause of health issues, though poor sleep, nightmares, depression and other mental problems that aren't easily explained may be caused by entity attachment. Since entities can usually be cleared using a simple statement of intention, it's often easiest to simply clear yourself and family members whenever they return from an outing. Of course, if you have multiple children in school, this can become a little more time-consuming, but for a few minutes' investment, you can help your kids concentrate, behave and sleep better.

If you know how to dowse, you can ask if a particular symptom is caused by entity attachment. If you don't dowse, just do a clearing of entities if you want to be sure this is not the cause. It never hurts to clear, even if you don't need it.

Whenever there are nightmares, it's safest to assume it's due to entity attachment and do a clearing. This is the one symptom that most often turns out to be related to entities, even though nightmares are not always due to entities.

Subconscious Beliefs & Health

Beliefs have a big effect on health and everything else in your life. Faulty beliefs usually lead to long-term health issues, because they have been in effect for a long time. It is less usual to have a recently activated belief affect your health, but it is possible. We recommend working to discover and clear long-held beliefs that may be affecting your health.

24

PITFALLS: STUBBORN SITUATIONS

In most cases, energy can be cleared by focusing your intention. Sometimes you need an anchor to help with that. You will find that energy generally clears rather easily if you employ proper technique. But some energies are harder to shift or transform. In this section, we will explore two of the most common stubborn types of energies to clear (curses and entities) and what you can do to improve your chances of resolving them.

∼

Active & Ongoing Curses

Active curses are blobs of ill-wish energy that are renewed on a regular basis. A curse that is not active is one that was hurled at you once and then never renewed by the sender. Road rage, minor annoyances and bad moods can lead to curses that are only sent one time. These are easy to clear. Active curses come from a source that is usually close to you and holds a strong grudge against you. An ex, a former business partner or an unpleasant in-law are examples of people who might send active curses to you. If your ex holds you responsible for depleting his financial resources and forcing him to get a second job, it is likely he is actively cursing you, because every day he has reminders of his plight, and he blames you. If your mother-in-law hates your guts, it is possible she is sending you curse energy on a regular basis, wishing her son would wise up and leave you, or that you would drop dead.

This type of curse can be disempowered over and over, and it will keep coming back as long as the sender has ill wish against you. That means you have to keep disempowering it, which is a pain. It also is not that effective at resolving the causes of symptoms you may be experiencing.

The most important fact to remember is that no one can affect you without your permission. A curse is going to affect you only if you have 'magnets' that attract it, or you have let down boundaries that protect you due to beliefs that let it come in. Here's an example: the belief that you must do what your mother tells you or wants, and that then translates subconsciously to doing what your mother-in-law wants. And if she wants you dead, you will end up becoming ill. These beliefs that lower your boundaries can be discovered and cleared. Most of these beliefs are about giving your power away, as in only valuing yourself as much as others value you, or trying to take away others' free will, as in wanting others to think a certain way about you instead of how they actually feel.

Magnet are balls of energy that resonate with the curse. We all have these. They are not intentional and don't mean that you are to blame for what you are experiencing, but it does mean that you have the opportunity to discover and clear those magnets, because they are not beneficial. When you give your power away or try to force others to think as you wish, you open the door to curse energy.

Examples of magnet energy are: victim, powerless, shame, judgment, worthless and other energies that would cause you to resonate with being harmed or judged. Get rid of those energies, and you are less susceptible to curses that resonate with them. We've all seen people who do rotten things and seem never to be affected by them, while on the other hand, kind people who are blameless suffer. This is due to their energies. If you can't or won't feel guilt or shame, someone can't make you feel it. Our society uses these emotions to control us, but they are detrimental to our happiness. You can be an ethical, kind person without feeling guilty and worthless.

The self-work and discovery that go along with disempowering active curses are very positive things. It will take time for you to find out the specific things acting on you, but in the end, you will make yourself safer and happier by doing so. This is a case of the journey being the main thing. Be patient and commit not to judging the person who cursed you. See the opportunity to become stronger in all ways. They won't have to change, and that's good, because you can never make someone else change unless they want to. The only person you can control is you.

Stubborn Entities

Most of the time, clearing entities is safe and easy when done properly. But there are a couple situations that can create difficulties. It is important that you be aware of these and act accordingly.

The more common situation occurs when entities perceive that a clearing is going to take place, and they leave the area or attach to something in the environment to avoid being cleared. A less common problem is when an entity is so noxious, that it is harmful to you if you try to clear it.

ENTITIES THAT FLEE

Most of the time, you won't have problems clearing entities. But some entities don't want to leave due to fear. They will either vacate the property or attach to a person, animal or object so that you cannot clear them. Dowsing is the only way to know for sure (and then, only if you are an accurate dowser) whether you have truly cleared all the entities that normally inhabit a space.

Dangerous Entities

Most human discarnates and many entities that are not human are safe and easy to move on to their right and perfect place. But some entities are such an energetic mismatch to humans that they are dangerous to come into contact with. If you are a highly empathetic person or lack strong boundaries, you could be harmed by trying to clear such entities.

The best way to avoid problems is to dowse ahead of time what the overall level in effects of doing the clearing will be on your health and well-being, using a +10 to –10 scale. Or ask if there will be any negative side effects to your doing the clearing, or if it is safe for you. Or ask if you have protection that is a 10 on a 0-10 scale. If you get any hint that it will be dangerous to you, DO NOT DO THE CLEARING. Find a professional who has experience in this subject and let them do the clearing.

25

PITFALLS: PERSONAL CHALLENGES

We are all imperfect beings, and the experiences we have are opportunities to make changes and become more genuine, less fearful and more fulfilled. When you engage in clearing work, situations may come up which highlight weaknesses or imbalances in you. Take the opportunity to do something about them, because it will help you be more effective at energy clearing. Some of the common issues that can affect your success are:

- Ego
- Fear of looking bad or being wrong
- Attachment to a particular outcome
- The need to judge something as good or bad
- The belief that being empathetic is 'good'; replace empathy with compassion
- Lack of practice or competence
- Lack of focus
- Lack of confidence
- Victim or powerless energy

We all have at least some degree of all of the above. Everyone is unique, so it behooves you to become familiar with your own weaknesses and deal with them using whatever method works best for you. We like energy techniques like tapping, especially the Emotional Freedom Technique (EFT), The Emotion Code and similar methods for helping shift unwanted emotions and beliefs.

Use your energy clearing activities as a part of your journey of personal growth. By becoming more authentic, confident and less judgmental, you will see improvement in your results when clearing energy.

26

PROTECTION

Whole books have been written on the topic of protection. It is beyond the scope of this book to repeat all the valuable information that is out there. Our goal is to alert you to the need for protection and to give you some tips.

No one is bulletproof. So you need to have protection when you are exposing yourself to noxious energies. But protection is only meant as a temporary fix. You should do your best to become stronger as time goes by, because protection can never be perfect. There is no method of protection that works in all situations.

To keep yourself safe, use common sense. Never do energy work when you are feeling sick, weak or negative. At those times, you are much more at risk for picking up noxious energies and entities.

Do protection before any session. Protection is achieved through your focused intention along with the application of any anchor that appeals to you or dowses as effective. The main ingredient is your intention to be safe during the time that you are doing the energy clearing. You can say a prayer, create a symbol, wear a color or crystal or call on angels and guides. Whatever you feel is best.

Depending on what you are working on, you may need extra or different protection. Do not just use the same type of protection all the time. Some situations will require extra strong protection. Dowsing is very useful in this regard.

As you become more energetically aware, you will notice if your protection drops during a clearing. You'll just get a feeling of a shift, like when you are not dressed warmly, and a chill breeze comes up. Stop what you are doing and dowse what your protection level is, and if you cannot dowse, just reapply the protection.

If you can't keep full protection, stop the clearing. It is vital to acknowledge your limitations. We have found that more empathetic individuals tend to be more at risk. There have been occasional times when Maggie could not get enough protection to do a job, but Nigel could. Rarely has it been the other way around. Maggie's boundaries are improving, but Nigel's have always been stronger. Nothing is more important than your health.

After you have done any type of energy work, clear yourself of any energies you might have picked up during the session. Taking the time to do this will keep you fit and safe.

27

SUCCESS STORIES

We did energy clearing of all kinds for a global clientele between 2000-2017, and we've gathered quite a few success stories from our clients. Rather than sprinkling success stories throughout the training, we have chosen to put them here, so that if you aren't of a mind to read them, it won't impact your absorbing the key content of this guide. However, it is very inspiring and builds your self-confidence when you read about the success of others. All of these stories are from real clients we have worked with in the past.

These stories have one thing in common: they tell of dramatic positive changes that occurred after energy was cleared. In many cases, the results were secondary to the original goal of the clearing, even at times totally unexpected.

∼

Total Behavior Changes

Improved behavior in humans and animals is a common result of energy clearing work. Space clearing or personal clearing can result in the transformation or removal of energies that were impacting the mood and behavior of the subject.

We did a space clearing on a ranch in another state. The woman reported to us that right after the clearing, a thunderstorm came up, and she was forced to catch and halter her horse, which was in a pasture far from the barn. She said that usually in such circumstances she needed assistance, because the horse was very sensitive to noise and chaos and would try to kick her. In this instance, the horse stood calmly in the thunder and lightning while she put the halter on him and led him back to the barn. She was nothing short of amazed. Apparently, either there were entities attached to the horse or noxious environmental energies that were causing it to act up.

In another case, we did a space clearing on a home for a client, and she reported that her sons, who were normally inclined to fight and create havoc, peacefully sat and did their homework without being threatened several times. She said this was very unusual for them, and she appreciated it.

Health Improvement

A client told us that after we cleared her home space, the sinus headaches she had suffered from for a long time disappeared. We had discovered a line of noxious energy in her bed approximately at her pillow. The same situation happened with Maggie as a result of sitting on a couch which had a negative line of energy running just in front of it. Her foot chakras began to close and cause great pain when she walked after sitting on the couch for a while. She had never had this symptom before, and it went away once the line was cleared, and it never returned.

A new client came to us due to major health issues. His doctor had refused to work with him, because the doctor was beginning to also have health issues. Our client was concerned he was cursed, and although that might sound outlandish, it turned out that he was cursed, and it was an active curse. It took a good deal of work to alleviate the symptoms, but over time, the situation improved noticeably.

Sleep Improvement

Children are particularly sensitive to entities, and in addition to behavior issues, they will often have nightmares if an entity is attached. This is so commonplace that a number of our clients would call for a space clearing based on nightmares showing up in their children. After the clearing, the children slept soundly. Always clear entities if there are unexplained nightmares.

An Elderly Dog's Passing

A client called to ask if we could assist in making the passing of her beloved dog easier. She didn't want to take her dog to the vet for euthanasia. In this case, all we did was clear energies and harmonize the dog so that he could pass easily if it was his time. (Don't assume anything, nor push for any particular outcome.) He went peacefully in his sleep within hours of the clearing.

Serious Mental Health Issues Disappear

We were asked to consult on a teenager who had suddenly gone from an honor student to mental disarray, panic and sleeplessness. The problems had been going on for several months, and the girl had recently had a fugue state and came back to reality in front of a knife block, knowing she was supposed to cut her wrists. She ran to the neighbor's, as her family was out, and asked for help. Her doctor said she had no signs of drugs, but she had been saying someone tried to kidnap her from school and that red eyes watched her at night, and he recommended she go for a mental evaluation. Before doing that, her mother wanted to try one last thing, because she was truly frightened that the only option was going to be to commit her and drug her.

Our dowsing indicated she had a very bad entity attached to her. Maggie could not get enough protection to participate in the clearing, but dowsing said that it was safe for Nigel. He did the clearing. The girl was unaware that the clearing had been done. Her mother reported the next day that her daughter had slept well for the first time in months that night, and she seemed so changed, that she put off the evaluation. Her daughter never saw red eyes at night again, never had another problem like she'd been experiencing, and went back to being a happy, well-balanced honor student. We even got a thank you card and a picture of her with her prom date.

What Else Might Happen?

Energy clearing can have just about any positive outcome, and you can't predict what will happen. New opportunities can appear, a windfall or increased income may manifest or cravings might disappear. When you restore harmony to a person or space, things just tend to go a lot smoother.

28

SUMMARY

If you are a newbie who has read this entire guide and done the exercises, you probably see energy clearing much differently than you did when you started reading. Maybe you thought you understood what energy and energy clearing were, but now you have a far more solid awareness of this complex, ever-changing subject. At first, maybe you thought that we'd give you a simple step-by-step process that would clear any type of energy all the time, but you discovered that is not possible. Perhaps you thought only a psychic could perceive and measure invisible energies, but now you know that you have powerful intuitive senses that can guide you, so that you aren't working blind, and that if you learn to dowse, you can know a lot of details about the energy you're clearing.

If you are a veteran of energy clearing and dowsing, you have learned the crucial fact that as energies change, your methods will need to change to stay effective, and the more tools you have in your toolkit, the easier it is to be effective. You know there are no magic bullets or rituals; the magic is in you, your focus and intention. You also are more in tune with the fact that what's 'out there' is a reflection of your own energy, so it is important to work on your own energy, so that you can see positive change around you. Lastly, you have been given a grounding in ethical practices and protection, so that you can avoid negative karma and harm to yourself when you clear energy. Perhaps most importantly, you have learned that you need to be aware of when to clear and when not to clear, and that not every situation is safe for you to get involved in, no matter how expert you are.

The goal of this guide is to give you a strong foundation in the principles of energy clearing and to allow you to grow and adapt as you practice this empowering technique. In the next section, we give a brief summary of the basic steps in the clearing process, so you can refer to them easily until such time as you have them memorized.

29

STEP-BY-STEP INSTRUCTIONS

This section is a summary of the key steps you need to follow in energy clearing. Refer to the appropriate chapter for details.

Step 1: Goals

Be very clear about **why** you are doing an energy clearing. You can't demand specific results, but you need to have a goal.

Step 2: Get Permission

Never do energy work without the verbal permission of the person involved, if it is not you or your space.

Step 3: Pick A Clearing Process/Anchor

Focus and intention are what you need in order to clear energy. Any method you use depends on intention for success. Intention often works best when anchored in some fashion during and even after the clearing. There is no single method that works for everyone, all the time. Energies require different treatments, and the person clearing is unique and will have varying results depending on personal energy. Use your intuition or dowsing to choose a method for each job.

Step 4: Get Protection

If you can dowse, dowse if you will be protected during the entire clearing at a 10 on a 0-10 scale, with 10 being total protection. If you do not dowse, tune in to the case and get a feel for whether it feels like something you are competent to do. Use protection before starting the clearing.

Step 5: Do The Clearing

Choose the appropriate clearing method and do the clearing. If you can dowse, check your results afterwards with dowsing.

Step 6: Clear Yourself Afterwards

Use whatever method dowses or feels appropriate to make sure you clear yourself of any energies you might have picked up or be influenced by as a result of the clearing.

How Do You Become Confident And Competent?

As with any skill, practice makes perfect. It is normal at first to doubt yourself. Try to measure the results in some concrete fashion. Look for changes, even changes you don't expect. Practice using your intuitive senses. Keep a journal with all the details and reread it from time to time. Make a note of how confident you felt on a 0-10 scale. Watch that number rise. Do self-work to rid yourself of victim and powerlessness energy. Shift your perception into a more empowered mode. You cannot become a powerful person if you are a victim or powerless in other areas of your life. Being an energy worker of any kind challenges you to grow as a person, and this can best be done by self-work using whatever methods you like best.

THE BUSY PERSON'S GUIDE TO SPACE CLEARING

BUSY PERSON'S GUIDES, BOOK 2

Copyright © 2018 Maggie & Nigel Percy

ISBN: 978-1-946014-25-2

All rights reserved. No part of this publication may be reproduced, distributed or transmitted in any form or by any means, including photocopying, recording, or other electronic or mechanical methods, without the prior written permission of the publisher, except in the case of brief quotations embodied in critical reviews and certain other noncommercial uses permitted by copyright law. For permission requests, write to the publisher, addressed "Attention: Permissions Coordinator," at the address below.

Sixth Sense Books

150 Buck Run E

Dahlonega, GA 30533

Email address: discoveringdowsing@gmail.com

INTRODUCTION

You're reading this book because you're interested in learning about how to clear noxious environmental energies at home or work using simple methods, but life keeps getting busier, and it's hard to find the time to read a bunch of books or take a course.

You just want to learn whatever you need to know so you can get started, no frills and no useless facts. But space clearing isn't as simple as 1-2-3. There is no single method that works in all situations, so anyone who only gives you a single, stepwise space clearing method (such as waving a sage wand around) has not done you a service.

In this guide, we give you a concise but solid foundation in what noxious environmental energy is, how it can affect you, and how you can transform it, as well as the knowledge you need to act ethically and safely while you do space clearing.

The subtle difference is the same as between 'give a man a fish' and 'teach a man to fish.' If we hand you a few step-by-step instructions for clearing your space, that would not allow you to grow into a masterful clearer of environmental energies. By giving you a foundation in energy, protection and ethics, as well as basic clearing methods, *The Busy Person's Guide To Space Clearing* will help you quickly become competent to do space clearing in all kinds of situations while allowing you to adapt to the ever-changing energy environment.

We must provide a warning, however. There is no way to endow you *instantly* with what you need to know. While our guide is as concise as possible, you will still have to read, digest and practice what we teach. And we encourage you to continue your education after you complete this guide.

Depending on your commitment, interest and how much time you have to devote, you can master the material in *The Busy Person's Guide To Space Clearing* in one intense weekend or a leisurely month of study. Either way, that's a remarkable achievement for so small an investment of time and money.

HOW TO USE THIS GUIDE

We've created *The Busy Person's Guide To Space Clearing* to be packed with all the information you need to become competent in space clearing, but you still need to commit to learning the material if you want to master it.

If you can find several hours to dive into the book, you can cover it in one intensive day. We think you'll remember it better and have more fun if you spread out the learning experience over a longer time period.

Most people can complete the book by spending as little as ten minutes a day for less than a month. So break it down into as many small chunks as needed to accommodate your schedule and attention span.

JUST FOLLOW **these steps to get the most out of it.**

Step 1: Don't skip any parts. There are no unnecessary sections. Each chapter builds on the previous one. If you're really busy, just do one section a day. Commit to doing that until you complete the book. Each section takes on average 10 minutes or less to complete.

Step 2: Do all the exercises. We suggest you get a journal or notebook to write your results in. You don't create competency by memorizing facts. You become masterful by applying what you have learned, by thinking deeply about it. Your participation is a unique aspect of these guides and helps you to learn faster.

Step 3: Get out and practice what you've learned and improve your life.

A Final Reminder:

Don't skip the exercises. Don't skip anything. The goal is not to see how quickly you can finish the guide; the goal is to master all the material in it, because only by doing that can you hope to become competent at space clearing.

1

WHAT IS SPACE CLEARING?

Space clearing is a term applied to a particular kind of energy clearing that relates to environmental energies. Historically, space clearing was done to remove detrimental energies from a person's environment. As time passed, people learned to *transform* energies to beneficial for all who lived or worked in a space. This intention later came to include the understanding that different species have different responses to any given energy, and that led to the goal of *harmonizing* the energy to be beneficial for all who lived, worked and visited in a space, whether human or animal, or even plants.

Environmental harmonization is actually a better term for this type of energy clearing, but the old name has held, so we will continue to use the phrase 'space clearing' throughout this guide. Just remember that you aren't simply 'clearing' or removing 'bad' energies; you are transforming the energies to be beneficial for all who occupy that space.

Space clearing can be performed on any space: residential, business, recreational, personal or public, with a few exceptions that relate to permission, which is discussed in a later section.

EXERCISE

In your journal, write down what particular space you want to clear. Your home? Your workspace? Your car? Make a note of why you want to clear this space. Are there any symptoms you are concerned about?

Are you interested in becoming a professional and clearing space for clients, or do you just want to do it for yourself and possibly your extended family?

How did you become interested in this subject? Did you have someone clear your space? Did you attend a presentation or workshop? What was that source's attitude about clearing space? Did the person say you have to remove bad energies? Did they say you have to move your bed or move to a new home if you have detrimental energies present? Or did they believe you can use anchored intention to transform any energy to beneficial? What methods did they suggest you use for space clearing?

Have you ever tried to clear a space? If so, what did you do, and what were the results?

2

WHY CLEAR YOUR SPACE?

Space clearing is as important, or perhaps more important, than regular housecleaning. You can tell your windows need washing or your floor needs vacuuming just by looking at them. The physical evidence of dirt won't be denied. But just like the dirt that accumulates at home and work, dirty energies pile up in any space, and they need to be cleared regularly, or they can affect your health and well-being as much or more than physical dirt does.

The problem is that energies are invisible, and all you can see is the physical consequences of them, and it isn't obvious what the causes are. In most cases, people assume that physical symptoms have physical causes, which is not always the case.

Noxious environmental energies can cause cancer. This has been scientifically proven. They also have been scientifically shown to cause measurable physiological changes in the body.

But energies have an effect on much more than your physical health. Energies affect your finances, your relationships and your mental/emotional health. If you run a business, energies can harm productivity, harmony among workers and profits. Environmental energies can impact your pets, even to the point of killing them.

Detrimental energies can make it difficult to sell your house. While studies have not been done on these topics, we have seen convincing proof during the many years we worked with clients around the world to harmonize their living and working space.

So you can see that your interest in learning to do space clearing could have a big impact: on your health and well-being, your relationships, your finances, your business and your pets.

3

SYMPTOMS OF NOXIOUS ENERGY

How can you tell there is noxious energy in your home or workplace? Humans, like other animals, have the innate ability to sense a lot about their energetic and physical environments. The first way to know that you might have noxious energy in your space is due to physical, mental or emotional symptoms.

Any type of symptom can be caused by noxious environmental energies, but some of the most common are:

- Disturbed sleep patterns and nightmares
- A sense of restlessness, fear or being watched
- Unexplained depression or OCD
- Extreme emotions that cannot be easily rationalized
- A desire to leave a place, though you don't know why
- A physical symptom that does not respond to treatment or that disappears when you go on a trip
- Cancer is often caused by noxious energies, especially geopathic ones
- Weeds or insects and other animal pests thriving (because they thrive on noxious energies)

- A dog who gets ill and doesn't respond to treatment, and the illness seems unusual for the age or condition of the dog

Life is busy, and for most people, popping an over-the-counter remedy or seeking a physical solution or just ignoring a problem and rationalizing that it's due to age or something like that is the normal reaction, but as a more enlightened person, you need to be open to the possibility that what you are observing might be caused by environmental energies.

If that is the case, clearing your space could eliminate or vastly reduce the symptom. Obviously, all of the above have many possible causes, but doing a space clearing is free, easy and worth taking the time to do if you can eliminate any of the above symptoms. If the symptom remains unchanged, then either you were unsuccessful in your clearing, or the cause is not environmental energies. It's that simple.

EXERCISE

Answer the following questions in your journal about your home.

- How do you feel about your home in general? Do you find it peaceful? Does it contribute to a sense of relaxation for you?
- Is there one particular place that you or someone in your family is afraid of or doesn't like to spend time in?
- Do you sleep well at night, or do you have nightmares or insomnia?
- Do your children have nightmares?
- Do you have a dog that has become ill to an extent that seems extreme, given the dog's age and how well you feed and treat it?
- Do you have any physical symptoms that disappear when you go on a trip?
- Do you have a lot of pests in your home or yard? Rats, mice, ants and wasps, for example.
- Do you have a lot of weeds in some areas of your yard? Do you

have any wild plants like burdock that are medicinal plants which thrive on your property?
- Do you or anyone in your family find it harder to concentrate at home than elsewhere?
- Have you struggled with depression or OCD since you moved to your home?
- Are you aware of any large transformers, cell phone towers or wifi sources close to your property?

All of the above can be indications of noxious environmental energies. We'll be explaining in more detail in later chapters, but make a note of those which you are seeing, note the frequency or intensity and how long you have been experiencing the symptom.

WHAT YOU HAVE LEARNED

Noxious energies can be the cause of many problems that you thought had other causes. Cancer, nightmares and depression can all be caused by energies in your living space. You have the power to transform dangerous environmental energies to beneficial and improve your life measurably.

4

EFFECTS OF NOXIOUS ENERGY

Detrimental environmental energy can wreck your health, business and finances. It can negatively impact your relationships and the behavior of your children and pets. It can make it difficult for you to concentrate, focus and accomplish what you want to do.

You can't expect to live a happy, healthy, abundant and harmonious life if you are surrounded by noxious energies. By definition, noxious energies have a bad effect on you, so it behooves you to create harmonious space in which to live and work.

Noxious environmental energy is not always the cause of problems in your life. In a later section, we'll give you tips on how to sense detrimental energies and even how to use a technique called dowsing to verify if your problems are caused by noxious energies.

No matter how your life is going, you will benefit from clearing your space regularly, just as you benefit from cleaning your house regularly. But there are some hints that the problems you are experiencing may indeed be caused by environmental energies. Here are the most common ways to tell you have problem energies in your space:

- The problem you are experiencing began when you moved to your home or began your job
- The problem disappears when you go on vacation
- The problem is not something you have had lifelong issues with
- You see a sudden and unexplained change in behavior, finances, health or some aspect of your life
- You feel very strongly that something isn't right (at home or at work), because you just can't relax and aren't at your best when you are in that space

∼

EXERCISE

In your journal, make a note of any of the above you have experienced, along with dates and relevant details. Don't be afraid to include things that are simply hunches or intuition.

5

TYPES OF NOXIOUS ENERGY

It can be useful to talk about noxious energies based on 'type,' because not all energies are the same, nor do all energies respond to the same method of clearing. There is no one method of categorizing that is best, but we have found it useful to list types of energies based on their origin.

Our system is just one of many possible systems, so feel free to modify it as you accumulate experience. Here are the types we use:

- Geopathic stress (earth energies)
- Manmade/human energies
- Cosmic energies
- Other

∼

Geopathic Stress

The type of detrimental energies most often addressed in space clearing presentations is geopathic stress, or noxious earth energies. These are known from ancient history and have been the best studied as relates to health problems like cancer. But they are only one type of noxious energy.

Human Energies

Manmade or human energies include conscious energies like curses, that originate with a human, and energies like wifi and other EMFs (electromagnetic fields) generated by human machines. Human discarnates (ghosts) also fall into this category.

Cosmic Energies

A type of noxious energies rarely addressed by space clearers is cosmic energies. Cosmic energies originate from outside the earth: from other planets, from stars, from alien beings, from other dimensions. These types of energies can be highly noxious and hard to clear, and it is important to include them in your space clearing process. As with human energies, cosmic energies can be conscious (as in coming from aliens with intent) or un-conscious, as in star energies. Nonhuman, non-terrestrial entities are included in this category.

OTHER

The category 'Other' is always needed to be sure that you haven't missed something. Whatever your system is, at some point, an energy may appear that doesn't fall clearly into one category or other. Perhaps it will be an energy that spans two categories by having elements of both. Or it could be something totally unlike the categories you set up. Using 'Other' as a category helps you to remember to think flexibly when you do space clearing work. You probably won't see a lot of things appearing in this category, but it's necessary for assuring your work is complete.

Having categories of energies helps you to think about environmental energy in new ways, as well as helping you to communicate with clients, friends and other space clearers. It is very useful to have a common vocabulary for good communication. You could name the energies by color or number if you wished, but then, it would only be meaningful to you.

These categories are particularly useful if you use dowsing during space clearing. Dowsing will be explained in a later section.

Cyclic Energy

Some energies become active, then go dormant, then reappear, and if you do a clearing while they are dormant, they usually are not transformed. Such energies are hard to detect while dormant, and we have found they explain some cases of noxious energies reappearing soon after a clearing. If you find that a clearing works, but not for long, check for cyclic energies and clear them while they are active.

There are many different types of noxious earth energies. (Of course there are earth energies that are beneficial to you, but we don't focus on them in space clearing. You would be smart, however, to focus on them when choosing where to live.)

Geopathic Energies

What follows is a description of common geopathic energies. Earth energies can be moving, moving in one direction, alternating back and forth along a line, stationary or whirling in a cyclonic pattern. There are no conscious geopathic energies. (We allow that the earth can be said to be conscious, but for purposes of space clearing, we are referring to consciousness of humans and other similar beings.)

Negative Lines Of Energy

Lines of energy are prevalent on the earth, and some have detrimental effects on humans. They vary in width, flow rate and direction. Some even flow like alternating current. A line can be narrow or wide. It can sit on top of the surface of the earth or be partially buried. Lines move in sinuous paths or straight, and they can end in a spiral or vortex or dive up or down.

Underground Water

Underground water produces energy due to friction as it moves through the earth, but even a still body of underground water can have a negative effect on humans living above it. Water has been shown to accumulate energies, so if you live downstream from negative energy sources, the water flowing underground may be full of negative energies it picked up from those locations. This is true of both physical toxins in the water and detrimental emotional energies.

It believed that dowsers can not only find underground water, but move water sources or attract them, depending on their intent. This is a manifestation of the concept that you in a sense participate in creating your reality, and that will be discussed in a later section.

Vortices

A tornado of energy is called a vortex. Vortices can be beneficial, detrimental or alternate from one to the other. A beneficial vortex, such as created by building a labyrinth, if not maintained, can turn to detrimental.

Vortices are powerful and can extend higher in the air than lines generally do. It is best to remove vortices regardless of their effect, unless you want to regularly do some practice that maintains it as beneficial.

Spots Of Negative Energy

Like a spill on the floor, you can find pools of noxious energy of all sizes and shapes on the surface of the earth, and they vary in thickness or how far they extend above the surface.

Radon Gas

Radon gas is a physical toxin that can contribute to ill health and is present in some areas.

FRACTURE LINES

The entire surface of the earth is wrinkled and cracked, but some fractures are actively moving, although at a very slow pace. Some fracture lines will generate noxious energy.

Human Energies

Every day, technology produces new types of manmade energies that have detrimental effects on humans, compounding the challenge of staying healthy. This partial list will give you some basic understanding about noxious human energies.

These energies can be classified into two types: conscious or not. By conscious, we mean the energy comes from a human being. By not conscious, we mean the energy is being emitted from machinery or instruments, or that it is discarded human stress energies that pile up in a place.

Human energies in general are more challenging to deal with than geopathic energies, in part because many of them are conscious and also because many of them are not natural.

CONSCIOUS MANMADE ENERGY

Curses

Curses are bundles of detrimental energy hurled at a person, place or thing. Usually, the negative effect of a curse diminishes over time. But if a curse has been initiated by a powerful person with great emotion and focus, it can last long after that person is dead. Such curses are not renewable, so once cleared, they do not come back.

The most challenging type of curse is an active curse, such as your ex gets up every day and curses you in some fashion. An active curse can return after clearing, because it is hurled again. While most curses can be cleared during a space clearing easily, an active curse will require you to find out what the magnets are within you that allow that energy to affect you, because you can't control what others do, but you can control your own energy.

This goes beyond space clearing, but can help you learn the complex relationship between your energy and that around you. A magnet is a belief or programmed attitude like one that says you must be a victim of someone or allow them to have their way, or that you are powerless, or that people are always hurting you. Once you clear the faulty belief, improve your boundaries and take your power back, the curse can't affect you any longer. This process usually takes time, and there is no one-size-fits-all solution, so you may need outside help.

Ghosts

Discarnates (beings who no longer have bodies) are often called ghosts if they are human. There are plenty of animal and human discarnates trapped in the physical plane. During a space clearing, you can help them move on to their right and perfect place. Many human discarnates hang around the earth plane due to fear of punishment, so if you find a stubborn ghost, in most cases if you assure it that it will not be punished, it will move along when cleared instead of trying to stay here.

Ghosts can attach to people, causing them to have symptoms or emotions similar to those the ghost had when in physical form. Discarnates can also cause mischief of various types, so it's good to help them move on.

Discarnates that don't want to be sent to their right and perfect place will run away before the clearing, then return afterwards. Or they will attach to a person, pet or large tree, which will secure them to the earth unless you focus on clearing people, pets and trees of attachments. Many clearing methods do not take these facts into account, and that makes them less effective.

Outside Influence

The media exists not to inform you, but to shape your thoughts and actions. It is wise to disconnect from the media as much as possible, because you will find yourself feeling unpleasant emotions like anger and fear while at the same time feeling powerless to change anything. That is actually one of the prime goals of media. Obviously, in our society, getting you to buy stuff is another influence the media has. The effect that is most harmful in general is inspiring fear, anger and a sense of powerlessness in you.

Working on boundaries and having a feeling of being a victor and being powerful is the antidote to much of this noxious energy, as most people cannot completely disconnect from outside influence. Meditating or regularly doing a practice that brings peace to you is worthwhile, as it makes you more bulletproof. Another behavior that is valuable is to question everything. Do not accept things just because you see them in the media. Especially question anything that is stoking fear or anger.

Un-Conscious Manmade Energy

EMFs

Electromagnetic frequencies (EMFs) are proliferating at an alarming rate, and they have a negative impact on health, yet few people are concerned, because the media isn't telling them to be afraid. We aren't suggesting you should fear EMFs, but you would be wise to educate yourself and limit exposure as much as possible.

EMFs come from electrical outlets, any source like a TV or computer (even when off), microwave ovens, smart phones, tablets, wifi and others. Keep all such devices out of your bedroom, because that is where you spend the most time. Eliminate clock radios and phone chargers from your sleeping area. Make sure you are not sleeping in a room that has the power company's smart meter attached on the outside wall. Switch from a smart meter to an analog one if possible. It's worth the small charge to be safer. Don't use a microwave oven, as it not only emits EMFs, it damages the structure of food. Convert your wifi to ethernet. It is faster and safer. Do not carry electronic devices on your person. Get rid of your smartphone and get a simple flip phone. Do not allow your children to use electronic devices any more than necessary, as the EMFs are more harmful to growing humans.

There will be wifi coming in from neighbors and challenges like cell phone towers you cannot control. How can you stop these from affecting you? Physical means are quite expensive and problematic to install at the time of this writing. Some people may have the ability to power their intention and block such EMFs. A meter will confirm if you have that ability, and how often you need to renew the 'fix' to block all of them. Sometimes you can use a crystal, an array of crystals, color or symbols to block EMFs. Dowsing is the best way to find a good method, and a meter is the only way to confirm you have succeeded. Never assume that you have fixed a major EMF problem. Look at symptoms to indicate whether you have succeeded, and use a meter to test levels.

EMFs are a big challenge, as they are proliferating and changing to more powerful versions. 5G is going to be an even bigger challenge than past systems. The key is not to be afraid, but to feel empowered to find the means to stay safe within your budget of time and money. A meter is a good investment for helping you find 'dirty' electric energy sources and to let you know how detrimental the EMFs are in your home. You can hire someone to come in and check or get a meter and do it yourself. There are reliable resources online who will recommend what brand and type to get.

Because the sources continue to emit EMFs, your best bet is to eliminate as many in your home as possible and do clearing as often as necessary, plus use whatever method resonates with you to block EMFs coming in from outside, if that is a problem in your area.

If someone in your family has health issues that seem odd or don't respond to treatment, consider checking EMFs, because electrostress is becoming an increasing source of ill health.

Stress Energy

An often overlooked source of detrimental energy is the energy of stress that piles up simply as a result of daily life. At home or at work, you are often under stress. Even if you aren't having a health challenge, going through a divorce or struggling to make ends meet, you will shed stress energies all day long. This is one reason to consciously do a practice to create peace within you, but most people don't feel they have the time.

You are affecting your environment with your emotions and your own energy. If you are at peace, you spread peace and harmony wherever you go. If you are struggling and stressed, you spread those energies. Get a few people living together, and the detrimental energies pile up like dust on furniture. Those energies have an effect on you. Regular space clearing will transform them just like vacuuming cleans your floors.

Cosmic Energies

Cosmic energies are the least discussed type of noxious energy, but if you ignore them, you will often fail to clear a place. Cosmic energies can be mild, moderate or very intense. They can be conscious or not conscious, just like manmade energies.

Cosmic energies come from outside the earth. Conscious cosmic energies are directed from a consciousness that is outside of the earth or non terrestrial in origin. Cosmic energies that are not conscious are not directed from a being, nor do they have an agenda, but they can be harmful to you.

The following is a sample of some of the more common cosmic energies.

Conscious Cosmic Energies

Entities

Non terrestrial entities are an example of conscious cosmic energies. Not all spirits are human or animal. There are spiritual beings from other dimensions and locations present on earth. Not all of them are detrimental, but in space clearing, we are only concerned with the noxious ones.

The detrimental entities can be a horrible mismatch energetically to humans, having very negative effects. For the most part, they have no agenda. In some rare cases, they may not even be aware you exist except as a bad smell to them.

A rare case where they do have an agenda is that certain of them try to 'boost' the energy of transition in humans by pushing them to death by suicide, thinking that transitional energy will get them where they want to go. As far as we have seen in the few cases brought to us, their tactics are unsuccessful, but deadly to the humans. In one case, the entity went from person to person in a small town trying again and again to get the results it desired, with no success. The humans affected all seemed to be vibrating with 'transitional' energy, and that seems to be what attracts this rare type of entity, which is focused on transitioning. (It should be stressed that this is the most extreme form of entity danger and is very rare.)

We believe that a certain percentage of cases of insanity are actually caused by entity attachment, and that clearing the entities can heal the human or improve their condition. If you have a family member who has mental illness and can get their permission, a clearing could be helpful. If someone has a mental imbalance, that will attract entities, so regular clearing is advised. This is not space clearing so much as personal clearing, but we do recommend you clear all people, pets and trees in your space of all attachments when you clear the space, to assure entities haven't lingered.

Do not approach non terrestrial entities lightly. Never approach with anger or judgment. If you can't get good enough protection, seek professional assistance.

Alien Energies

Alien energies that are directed at a location or person or group of persons from a non terrestrial being are very real and can have any level of effect. An alien is a non terrestrial being. There are plenty of them around, and while not all are negative in their effects, some of them are. Experiments usually cover wide areas, and you can opt out of them, but caution is a good idea, as you do not want to attract attention.

Not all aliens regard humans as advanced beings. To some of them, we are no better than lab rats. Makes you reconsider the ethics of using animals for experiments, doesn't it?

Do not fear alien energy. It is true they may be more technologically advanced, but you still have free will and the right to live as you choose. Fear of aliens will only attract negative outcomes.

Un-Conscious Cosmic Energies

Star Energy

Energies emanate from stars. Sometimes these energies are detrimental to humans. They are not aimed at you or anyone in particular.

Historical Alien Energies

Energies can linger from historical events involving aliens. A single clearing will usually eliminate them.

Portals

Doorways to other dimensions, times and places can open just about anywhere, and often, entities are dumped into a place as a result. Closing the portals is a good idea.

Spirit Tracks

Spirit tracks are like subways for spirits. When a track gets broken, it can dump spirits into your location, and that piles up noxious energies. Repairing the spirit track and/or moving it outside your living space is the best remedy.

Astrological Energies (Universal)

Universal or astrological energies affect everyone on earth, but in different ways based on personal energy. There are also energies unique to a particular location in the universe as we travel through it on our planet. It is difficult if not impossible to transform such energies. Being aware that sometimes an energy effect is a universal one you cannot change can help you realign your approach to minimize problems.

6

NOT EVERYONE IS AFFECTED THE SAME

I f you want to be good at space clearing, you need a more nuanced viewpoint on energies than just finding and transforming 'bad' energy.

Energy isn't 'good' or 'bad' except as it relates to a certain species. Then it gets labeled based on its overall effect. But not every species has the same energy requirements, so what's bad for most humans can be beneficial for cats. And within a given species, not all individuals will react the same to a certain energy. Some will be more affected than others.

Space clearing is usually approached from the viewpoint of human health and well-being. That is great, but not all humans are alike in their response to environmental energy, and things get really complicated when you start including pets and plants into the mix, because they don't all react the same to a given energy. The main point is that energy itself just 'is.' It isn't inherently good or bad, and you need to approach it from that perspective.

You can often gain useful information by observing your environment using this awareness. Here are a few examples of how you can 'read' the energies in an environment by knowing the reactions of a species to certain energies and by reading the signs.

- Cancer is often a reaction to noxious earth energies. A string of cancers in a location often indicates detrimental energies. Not every human in a 'bad' location will get cancer, as each person is unique, but pay attention to patterns of illness.
- Trees will often bend away from energies that are harmful to them. If they cannot avoid noxious energy, you may see knots or other growths on the trunk of the tree. If you look at a group of trees, you can sometimes trace the path of a negative line of energy based on how the trees look and which ones have growths or extremely bent postures.
- Colonial insects like termites, ants, wasps and bees thrive in energies that are noxious to humans. Many plants we call weeds do the same. Pests (weeds, rats, ants) often indicate the presence of noxious energies (for humans), which is why using pesticides only makes things worse. The critters and plants are utilizing that energy. If you remove them, who is going to process it? Your compost pile will thrive on energy that is negative for humans, because it relies on microbes to do the work, and they like energy that is detrimental to humans.
- Clutter, trash and toxic waste is a sign of stagnant and detrimental energy (again, from the human standpoint).
- Cats find certain energies beneficial that are harmful to humans. This may be one reason that witches and other practitioners of the occult had cats as familiars, because the cat could process energies detrimental to the witch and not be harmed, providing a level of protection.
- Dogs and pigs react much the same as humans to environmental energies, so if your dog is ill, it is possible the energies in your environment are detrimental to both dogs and humans. In some cultures, houses were once built on locations that pigs would choose to settle on.
- Medicinal plants (many of which are termed weeds, like dandelion) thrive in areas of energy that are noxious to humans. They process the noxious energies/find them

beneficial, which might explain their beneficial effect on human health.

If you have pets or other family members living with you, you might want to check out the energies for each individual. This is where dowsing scales really help. A simple 'yes' or 'no' doesn't give you degrees of intensity, so we use either a 0-10 scale or a +10 to -10 scale. When looking at environmental energies, you can use a +10 to -10 scale to show how negative and how intense they are. A -10 is horribly detrimental, but a -3 is mildly negative. Just dowsing if there is noxious energy and getting a 'yes' won't give you this kind of information. When you consider that individuals differ in their reaction to energies, what is a -3 for you could be -8 for your dog or -7 for your child. Dowsing is the best way to get an accurate measure of the effects of an energy other than just getting a feeling for how healthy and happy the individual is, and we cover it in a later section.

Even if you cannot dowse, it is wise to be aware of individual reactions. If your child is afraid to go into the basement, don't dismiss that fear. It could be that your child is more aware of or sensitive to noxious energies present there. If your dog is ill, and nothing seems to help, it is possible your dog is 'taking on' noxious energies to protect you from them. We have seen this happen, and it is very dangerous to the dog's health.

Awareness of the spectrum of reactions of different family members, pets and plants will help you get a more intelligent and wiser outlook on space clearing. You will understand why we use the term environmental harmonization. Your goal isn't to find and clear 'bad' energy; your goal is to harmonize the energies to beneficial for all who live, work and visit there. If you focus on only creating energy beneficial to humans, your medicinal herb garden or cat might suffer.

What You Have Learned

Just looking at how environmental energies affect you and getting rid of 'bad' energies is not necessarily going to help all the people, pets and plants who live on the property. You can use dowsing to see how individuals and species are affected by the energies present. When you do your 'clearing,' you will be seeking to transform the energies to beneficial for all who live, work and visit there. How is it possible when the energy requirements are so varied? Intention is the key. What you intend is what will happen. We'll go into this in more detail later.

7

HOW TO SENSE NOXIOUS ENERGIES

Some people can sense energies easily. Others, not so much. When you sense energies, you will sense them in ways unique to you and your own talents and sensory capabilities. Even if you are not naturally sensitive to energies, you can learn to improve your abilities. So don't fret if you think you are 'blind' to energies.

All humans have physical senses. One person might be very visual and have great acuity. Another might hear sounds only a dog can perceive. A third person might be able to smell fragrances no one else can. The same is true of your intuitive senses. Most of us have not trained our intuitive senses, and that leaves them weak and unreliable. By learning to do space clearing, you can strengthen and engage your intuitive sensing abilities. That will be a benefit in all areas of your life.

Your strongest intuitive sensing ability may relate to your strongest physical sense. For example, if you are highly visual, you may have the ability to be clairvoyant about energies. Nigel is highly visual, and to him, noxious energies often appear as a gray cloud, like smoke. On the other hand, I tend to be more clairaudient or clairsentient. So I might hear entities as strange knocking noises at night while I'm trying to sleep. Or I just don't feel good when I am standing in a zone of noxious energy.

The trick is learning to recognize and credit your intuitive senses, so that they grow stronger. Here are some tips:

- Slow down and don't multitask. It's hard to notice subtle things when you are rushing or juggling a lot of priorities.
- If you see something out of the corner of your eye or feel something you can't explain, stop and tune into it. Try to memorize how you feel so you recognize it the next time you get that feeling. Make a note of what you are doing and where you are and try to see patterns.
- Trust your gut. Intuition is NOT a rational, linear process. You won't be able to convince someone else that what you felt was 'right.' It doesn't matter. The only person who has to believe you is you. Trust what you feel. Follow through on what your heart says. Make notes in your journal and watch how your intuitive sensing improves.
- Don't share your newfound perspective with skeptics. If you get involved in trying to persuade someone to your point of view, it can become frustrating and rarely creates the outcome you desire. Allow everyone to believe as they wish. If they are skeptics, bless them and move on.
- Put yourself into a position often where you get a chance to practice tuning in to energies. Practice makes perfect. Make notes of what you sense, and later go back and see if you can show you were correct. Being right isn't the main thing, but confirming your senses will build confidence.

∼

Exercise

Answer the following questions in your journal. Do you consider yourself sensitive to energies? What is your reaction to noxious energies? Do you 'see' them, 'feel' them, 'hear' them? Is there a pattern to your reactions that could help you with space clearing? Remember, you may react to different types of energies differently.

If you consider yourself unable to sense energies, practice slowing down the pace of your life and take time to just tune in to the energies at home and work. Spend quiet time in different rooms and see if you feel differently. Do this in locations you spend lots of time in: your bed, your favorite chair, etc. Are there areas you tend to avoid spending time in? Even if you aren't sensing anything, avoidance is often a sign of detrimental energies. You may rationalize such feelings, but in reality, you are probably aware at some level that they are noxious.

What You Have Learned

Being able to sense invisible energies is a natural part of your sensing array as a human being, but you haven't had the chance to develop and strengthen your intuitive senses. Be patient and take the time to tune in and discover your unique strengths for sensing the invisible energies in your environment. It isn't a psychic ability; it's natural. But you need to practice to hone your skill.

8

DOWSING ENERGIES

Dowsing is a natural human skill for getting answers to questions your brain can't answer. Think of dowsing as focused intuition. Instead of waiting for an intuitive hit, instead of 'tuning in' to a place and waiting for some sense of energy, you can dowse what's going on in any given space.

Why bother learning to dowse if you intend to clear space? Dowsing will tell you what the level in effects of the energy in a space is. The level in effects is a measure of how it is affecting you. You can use a +10 to -10 scale, with negative numbers meaning the energy is detrimental to you, and get a clear reading of the overall effects. You can also use dowsing to measure the level of individual energies in your environment, plus you can discover exactly what energies are present using dowsing.

Even if you hone your intuitive senses to a fine edge, you won't easily be able to tell if a detrimental energy is cosmic or a curse. While all that matters is that you can effectively transform the energy, it can give you confidence if you can dowse details. It is especially useful if you are working for clients. You need some way of communicating about what you found, and dowsing allows you to speak in a scientific fashion.

You don't have to dowse to clear space, but if you are able to dowse, you will find you are able to do much more, and it will be a better learning experience, too. Dowsing expands your intelligence and gives you answers your brain can't. We urge you to include dowsing among your many tools, because it is so applicable to many situations.

9

DOWSING BASICS

The power of dowsing is that you can use it to answer any question your mind can't answer. So when you want to know more about the energies in your home, dowsing is a perfect technique to use, either to identify energies and their effects or to pick the best method to clear them.

This guide is not a dowsing course. We have another guide on developing your intuition and a link to our dowsing course in the Resources section. We urge you to get that guide at least, because your intuition is a valuable resource. Don't let it sit unused, like a Ferrari in your garage covered by a tarp.

Learning to dowse is very straightforward, but like any skill, dowsing has complexities, and you will get better results if you get good training. What follows is just a taste of what is involved in dowsing, so you can decide if you want to plunge in and learn how to do it. Without dowsing, you won't be able to get much detail when space clearing. We strongly urge you to learn how to dowse.

Dowsing involves several steps:

1. Be clear about your goal

2. Form a question that is very detailed and specific and has a yes or no answer
3. Focus on the question and empty your mind (this is called getting into a dowsing state)
4. Be curious but not attached as to what the answer is
5. Receive the answer

Steps 1-4 seem pretty easy to understand, though I must warn you that each one involves work and practice to master. Make a mistake at any step, and your answer will probably be incorrect.

Step 5, the actual answer, is just a small part of the process, but it may be the part which is most unfamiliar to you. When you dowse, you can either use a tool like a pendulum, or you can dowse without a tool, using some part of your body to give you the answer (the latter is what kinesiologists do).

There are many methods of deviceless dowsing, but one of the most common and reliable is the Body Sway. The Body Sway uses the forward or backward motion of your body to indicate 'yes' or 'no.'

Give it a try. Stand straight, relaxed, feet shoulder width apart. Close your eyes. Breathe normally. Think of the city or country you were born in. Ask, "Was I born in _____?" (Fill in the blank with the correct answer.) Wait in a curious and detached way to see what your body does. Forward is usually 'yes.' Did you get forward motion?

Don't be upset if you did not. Maybe your 'yes' is backward motion. Check out your 'no' answer by doing it again, but this time, insert an answer you know is wrong for your birthplace. As long as you get a different motion for 'yes' and 'no,' you can dowse and get an answer.

Accurate dowsing depends on how good and clear your question is, how detached yet focused you are and a number of other factors we won't go into here, but are covered in our dowsing course.

The purpose of this demonstration was to show you that it is possible to tap into your intuition in a focused way and get an answer to a question right now. We used your birthplace, because it's easy, and you know what is right and wrong. When you actually dowse in the real world, you won't know if your answer is right or wrong, which is why we urge you to take our course, because it goes into detail about proper technique.

Scales are used in dowsing to go beyond yes/no answers and find out the level of intensity of a noxious energy. There are many kinds of scales, but 0-10 and +10 to -10 are most common. Finding out a number value consists of asking what the intensity is and either saying each number until you get 'yes,' using a chart that shows the numbers, or just thinking the numbers in your head and going through them as a list until you get a 'yes.'

It is important to take a good dowsing course if you want to be an accurate dowser. See the Resources for links to our course.

Exercise

You're going to determine the overall level in effect of the energy of your home on you at this time by dowsing.

Look at the 5 steps of dowsing and take your time. Write down what you do at each step. Write your goal down. Write down your question. Describe how you felt during steps 3 and 4. What answer did you get?

Use the Body Sway to discover the overall level in effects on you of the energy in your home at this time, using a +10 to -10 scale, with 0 being neutral. Here's a good sample question:

On a +10 to -10 scale, with negative numbers meaning detrimental, what is the overall level in effects on me of the environmental energies currently present in my home (or at work, if you want to test your workplace)?

Empty your mind, relax and be curious about the answer. While keeping the question in mind (and nothing else), say each number on the scale in turn until you get a 'yes' response (-10, -9, -8, -7, etc.) The biggest challenge will be to remain focused on your question during the process.

Double check the answer by asking if the overall level in effects is the number you got. (Sometimes a number will pop into your head if you are really dialed in. If that happens, dowse whether it is the correct answer, but be sure not to be attached to being 'right.')

You can make the question easier by asking this:

On a +10 to -10 scale, is the overall level in effects on me of the environmental energies in my home at this time -8 or worse?

That is a simple yes/no question, and -8 is the cutoff in our system for very serious energies that can have a bad effect and need immediate clearing. You can use any other number you want. -3 or less is mild, -4 to -7 is moderate, and -8 to -10 is serious. In other words, you can get a 'no' for the above question and still have noxious energies present.

Does your answer confirm what you intuitively felt? If not, do you feel comfortable with the answer you got? Does it make sense? Does it feel right to you? Either way, this exercise shows you that dowsing has huge potential, and that being able to dowse accurately is a powerful tool for doing space clearing.

You can also use dowsing to determine what types of energies are affecting you, how strong they are, what clearing method is best and to confirm they are cleared after you do your clearing.

10

INTENTIONS, GOALS, FOCUS

To create any kind of change, you need to have clear goals, intention, focus and then take right action. If you take action without intention or focus, your results may be very disappointing.

Here's an example: many people work out, or go on a diet, or follow a spiritual or religious regimen. But most of them are not doing anything consciously, meaning with focused intent. They are ticking a box on their 'to do' lists, and that makes them feel good, but for best results, you need to have a clear goal and focused intention as you take right action.

What are your goals for clearing a certain space? Here are some possible ones:

- Creating harmony so you feel peaceful
- Creating a healthy living space
- Improving relationships
- Enhancing good behavior in children and pets
- Improving finances
- Increasing productivity at work
- Improving focus and concentration

These are just a few goals you might have. If you have a very clear picture of harmony as an energetic environment which contributes to better health, attracts abundance and promotes creativity, etc., then you have all the bases covered. But it's OK to work for one particular goal if you wish. We tend to look at the big picture, but you can choose your own goals.

Be sure to include not just you, but all members of your family, your pets and those who visit.

When you are clear about what you want to create by clearing space, then you focus your intention to accomplish that. The method you use to transform the energies is a way to anchor your focused intention, so it's important to use a method that feels right to you. We'll discuss that in a later chapter.

Because focus is a vital part of the clearing process, do not attempt to perform space clearing with an audience or a lot of distractions, at least at first. You will get better results if you aren't answering questions, dealing with skeptics or having to block out distractions like loud noises, conversations or TV.

11

PERMISSION

The concept of ethics is a vital part of any type of healing or energy clearing and transformation. Sadly, this subject is not addressed in most courses. There is a general assumption that if your intentions are 'good,' then anything you do is appropriate and right.

You know what they say about the road to hell being paved with good intentions...

We assume that you have very good intentions for wanting to become a competent space clearer, but you also need a foundation in ethical practices, so that you don't create negative karma for yourself, so that you avoid acting out of ego, and so that you maintain good relationships with others, even those with different belief systems.

How Could I Possibly Create Negative Karma?

You can't create any negative karma for yourself by clearing your own space. But if you presume to clear space that is not yours without permission, simply because you value space clearing, that invades the privacy of others. It's like going into someone's house and vacuuming, because it's dirty and you think it should be clean. You would never do that, because it's a violation of privacy to do so without being asked. Clearing energies is the same thing.

If you invade another person's energy or space without being asked, then you have overstepped boundaries, and that will attract situations in your own life where people fail to respect your boundaries. Most of us are very sensitive when our boundaries are ignored, and with good reason. We work hard to create the life we choose, and we want our choices to be respected, even if others disagree with them.

So, avoid negative karma and life lessons. Respect the privacy of others, and do not under any circumstance perform a space clearing on their space unless they ask you to do so.

Can I Just Ask Permission Of Their High Self?

This is a workaround to asking permission directly, most often used when the person doing the clearing is afraid to ask, knowing they will likely be rejected. If you don't have the courage to offer to do a space clearing, don't do it. If you know the person is likely to laugh at your offer or reject it, don't turn to their 'High Self' as a way around it.

Very early in my career of energy work, I used this technique to clear a person of energy without their permission. I got instant results, but the situation I was working on immediately reverted back within a short time. I realized this meant that I had overridden the free will of that person, and that it was unethical to do so. I have never worked on anyone or any place without verbal permission since then.

Working on someone or a space without permission will not have long-term positive results, as free will always reinstates the status quo.

You Wouldn't Want Your Free Will Overridden

While most people do not live consciously, we all have free will. Free will gives us the right to create the life we choose. If we do not consciously choose, our lives tend to follow our subconscious beliefs and programming. At any time, we can decide to be conscious creators, but it is a challenge.

Whether you are consciously creating your life or not, how would you feel if someone tried to change you without permission? What if they could get you to temporarily hate chocolate or alcoholic beverages? What if they could instill an addiction to yoga in you? Even if the changes they made lasted or were considered healthy, how would you feel about not having a say in the process?

You may think a glass of wine at night or a juicy steak is good. There are others that feel they are evil. How would you feel about being forced to adopt a new viewpoint? Forced change does not persist, and it is an unethical thing to do.

What Is The Ethical Way?

If you are clearing your own home or workspace, you don't need permission. But to clear your neighbor's home or the entire building you work in, you need the appropriate person to give permission. The only ethical way to get permission is to ask the owner of the business or property. If the building you work in is a hospital or owned by a corporation, then get the permission of someone who can speak for the owners.

When you clear your workspace, clear it just for you, and it won't have any effect on others, so you don't need permission. If the business owner gives permission to clear the entire building, the free will of other workers can still refuse to submit to positive changes, but overall, it will probably improve things.

What if the property is part of a national park or federally owned, like a junction along an interstate highway? It's going to be very hard to get permission for clearing properties that are government-owned. It is difficult to find someone in charge to give you permission, but if you can find someone, it's OK to do.

~

What If You Can't Get Permission?

There will be places you can't get permission to clear. Sometimes, the lack of permission is a way of protecting you from noxious energies that would harm you, that are beyond your ability to deal with. Other times, it's a life lesson for you to learn that you can't always get what you want.

~

Exercise

Think very carefully about the principles explained above. Note in your journal whether you feel you are OK to clear under the following conditions or not. Please also note why you made your choice and note any specific details that relate to carrying out your choice.

- You feel certain that your uncle's cancer is probably due to geopathic stress, because the property he lives in has a long history of cancer cases. But he doesn't believe in space clearing. You are even afraid to broach the topic. You want your uncle to be healthy. Is it OK to clear his space without asking his permission?
- There is an intersection a few miles from where you live that has had repeated fatal accidents. You don't travel that way yourself, but you'd like to help out. Is it OK to clear that public space without asking permission of anyone?
- There is an intersection a few miles from where you live that has had repeated fatal accidents. You travel that way yourself often, and you'd like to help out and be safe. Is it OK to clear that public space without asking permission of anyone? Are there any specifics of the clearing that you need to do to make it ethical?
- You are going to be visiting a park or public area that has a

dreadful history of war, slaughter, massacre or torture. You would like to help make that space nicer and safer for you. Do you have the right to clear it without getting permission from someone?
- Your brother is in a coma after a terrible car accident. You know that hospitals are not healthy places in terms of environmental energy. You'd like your brother to recover and heal quickly. You only want to clear the room he is in for the duration of his stay; you're not trying to alter the overall energy of the entire hospital. He can't communicate with you. Is it OK for you to clear his room, even though he cannot speak with you about it?

WHAT YOU HAVE LEARNED

Power comes with responsibility. You need to think about ethical behavior and be able to explain your point of view when it comes to the topic of permission. There may be rare occasions when it's OK to clear space without permission, but they are very rare indeed and must adhere to the general principles described above. Using your ability ethically will help you get along with others, be a good learning experience about the use of power and create good karma for you.

12

PROTECTION

It's really exciting to do healing work, energy clearing or space clearing. But, too often, the dangers of such activities are overlooked, and that can be harmful to your health. We've seen people excited about being 'ghostbusters' go out with virtually no training, trying to contact discarnates and other spiritual entities. This practice is like playing with a loaded gun without any instruction about safety.

Space clearing is first and foremost a dipping into energy that is not 'you.' This may sound strange. You could say, "I live at home surrounded by those energies every day, so how could it be dangerous to clear them?" For the most part, on your own home territory, you are safe tuning in to the energies present. The occasional exception is certain types of 'conscious' energies, energies that originate from a human or alien source, or entities that have consciousness. By engaging them, you can find yourself in a dangerous situation.

You wear a raincoat when you go outside in the rain if you want your clothes to stay dry. If you want your hair to stay dry, you wear a hood or use an umbrella. This is a type of protection from the rain. Protection is not always perfect. You can have good rain gear, and the weather could be so windy that the rain still drips down your neck or gets your clothes wet. Or you step in a puddle, and your shoes get soaked. The more protection you have, the less likely you are to get wet, but it's a bit of a nuisance wearing a lot of extra clothing, even if you can afford to buy it.

Protection Is Never Perfect--Become 'Bulletproof'

As with protecting yourself from the rain or cold, no amount of protection you do before and during space clearing is going to be 100% all the time. So, regard protection as a necessary evil, but work towards making yourself as bulletproof as possible.

How can you do this:

- Take measures to improve your own energetic boundaries
- Reduce empathy, which is not a good thing, as it causes you to pick up negative energies
- Replace empathy with compassion, which doesn't require you to take on someone else's energies
- Acknowledge the right of free will to all people, even those you disagree with
- Work on yourself to reduce fear using whatever method you like best

Over time, if you accomplish the above, you will be less susceptible to the effects of detrimental energies.

Meanwhile, Use The Best Protection You Can

It is a journey to become less susceptible to other energies, so use protection before each space clearing to keep yourself as safe as possible. Being able to dowse accurately is the best way of choosing protection that will work, but even if you cannot dowse, you can learn to use your intuition to stay safe.

How To Protect Yourself

Using the same protection for every job is a mistake. The energies, even at your home, will change over time. Sometimes they will be mildly detrimental to you; other times, they will be very noxious. If you blindly use the same protection every time, sooner or later, you will find yourself in a bad situation.

What happens if you are not protected properly? You might have an entity attach to you. You might take on certain energies. You could be affected by a curse that isn't even pointed at you.

When such things happen, you could find yourself very ill. Noxious energies can affect your mental/emotional or physical health dramatically. They can also have an impact on finances and relationships, on work performance and well-being in general. You want to avoid being affected by the energies you intend to clear or transform.

There are many methods of protection:

- A prayer of intention, which is a statement asking to be protected during the entire process, should be detailed and clear and said with focused intent
- An amulet that you believe offers protection, such as a certain crystal, can help
- Symbols, colors and even fragrance can be used for protection
- You can use a combination of any of the above, or anything else that you believe offers protection

How do you choose the protection? Dowsing is the most foolproof way, but if you cannot dowse, then focus on the job you are going to do, the location you are clearing, and ask if you can use a method you know that will keep you protected 100% during the entire process. Be very clear about what you mean by protected. Have a list of methods available to you and slowly scan the list with that question in mind, and see which method or methods 'jump out' at you. Use them.

Sometimes, during a clearing, you can feel your protection drop out. It is a subtle sort of feeling that you have to learn to recognize. If you lose protection during a clearing, stop the clearing and restore the protection immediately. Do not wait. Dropped protection is usually a sign of very noxious energy.

If You Can't Stay Protected, Don't Do The Clearing

One of the hardest things is NOT exercising your power. Space clearing is a power, and you will sometimes find that you are not up to the task of clearing a certain space. This is *always* for your own protection, and you must not allow ego to cause you to proceed with a clearing if you cannot be fully protected. That will cause an unpleasant life lesson! (This won't happen when clearing your own home as a rule.)

Exercise

Have you ever used any form of protection? Prayer, an amulet, a color, a symbol? Do you ask for help in protecting yourself from your guides or angels? Any of these can be a great way to protect yourself. How can you tell that you are protected, if you are not a dowser? Do you just assume that you are protected, or can you 'feel' levels of protection? Have you ever felt your protection fail during a healing or clearing process? How could you tell?

You will find that you are most protected when you use methods that you believe in, so don't just do what others say to do; make sure that you believe in a method before using it. Experiment with different methods and note in your journal how you feel when you use them.

What You Have Learned

While most of the time, the energies in your home are not going to harm you during the clearing process, when doing clearings at work or on other properties, you will benefit from using protection to avoid negative effects to yourself. Protection is a stopgap measure while you work on yourself to become less affected by energies.

It is wisest to always use some form of protection before any clearing, and don't just use the same form all the time, as energies change, and you will need different protection at different times. Dowsing is the best way to choose effective protection.

13

HELPERS

It can be kind of scary when you first begin to do space clearing. So much of what you do is invisible, it's hard to get physical proof of results. You may find you doubt yourself about what you are sensing, whether you are effective and if you are dowsing accurately. All of this is a normal part of the process as you learn to clear space. You will gain in confidence as you see the results.

Another thing to think about is that you are not alone in this undertaking. There are many spiritual helpers you can turn to. Knowing that you have help will build your confidence, and your helpers will improve your results.

As with protection, what helpers you choose will depend on your belief system. If you don't believe in angels, don't turn to them for help. If you prefer, you can work with your guides. Some people like to work with the fairies, especially in natural environments. Nature spirits and fairies can be very helpful in the outdoor spaces.

The time to contact your helpers is before the clearing, before you even begin to try and sense energies. Do your protection and ask your spiritual helpers for their assistance in staying protected and reaching your goals for the clearing.

Also, you might want to ask them to give you a sign if it isn't safe for you to do the clearing. This is unlikely to be the case if you are clearing your own living space, but may be the case if you are clearing space you don't live in.

You are not required to ask for help when space clearing. It is personal preference based on belief. Use your own judgment. Don't do things simply because someone else does them.

Be very clear whom you are asking for help. There are plenty of advanced beings 'out there,' and not all of them are compatible with human health and goals. If you just ask for any kind of help, you may not like the form it comes in. So be specific when asking for help.

You will grow as you learn. You can also 'outgrow' certain types of help. It is unlikely that you will follow the same exact space clearing procedure all of your life. Be flexible. Don't feel like there is only one right way to perform space clearing, and remember that what works for you is for you, and it is not the only right way to clear space.

WHAT YOU HAVE LEARNED

Getting help during space clearing is not a requirement, but it can make you feel more confident of your results. Don't do things by rote; follow your own beliefs. Allow yourself to change over time.

14

HOW OFTEN TO CLEAR

One of the most common questions people ask after learning space clearing is, "How often should I clear my space?" This is a very good question, but there is no single right answer. As a general rule in 2018, once a month for work space and once a quarter for home is an average frequency. If you are going through a lot at work or home, more frequent clearings will be needed. And remember that energies change over time. Years from now, less frequent or more frequent clearing may be the rule. Be flexible.

When is monthly clearing not enough for your workspace?

- If you work in a high-stress situation or one where there is a lot of negative energy. Health care and prisons would be two obvious situations where more clearing is needed for best results.
- If you work in a high-traffic environment. The more people you interact with each day, the more energy gets dumped in your workspace. Even if you aren't interacting with them, if there are lots of people going through the area you work, it will need more frequent clearing.
- If your workspace is located in a toxic environment or one surrounded by icky energies, you will need to clear more often.

City environments and locations adjacent to dumps and toxic waste are examples.
- If you have a toxic work situation with lots of negative people, either coworkers or bosses, more frequent clearing is needed.

When is quarterly clearing not enough for your home?

- If you are going through a highly stressful time, like a divorce, job loss or health problem, clear more often.
- If you live in a high-density environment, like an apartment building, you will need to clear more often.
- If your home is located in a toxic neighborhood, with lots of crime or a cell phone tower or industry nearby, you will need to clear more often.

As you can imagine, these factors will change over time. Quarterly clearing of your home may be perfect now, but when you take on the care of your aging parents, you may need to clear every month. Be open to re-evaluating your situation and don't get into a rut.

EXERCISE

Think about the space you want to clear. Using the above criteria, do you think that the average clearing frequency is adequate to your needs? If not, why not? If so, why so? Make notes in your journal. Do NOT do what many people do and ignore the stresses in your life. Face them so that you can clear as often as needed to get good results. It isn't weak to admit life is stressful. It doesn't mean you are a failure. We all go through tough times, and being honest is the best way to improve things.

15

SPACE CLEARING "TOOLS"

When we talk about space clearing methods, we are referring to physical anchors and actions that signal your intent to create harmony and well-being through the clearing process. Later, we give you a step-by-step list of what to do, but here, let's talk about the many different ways you can effectively clear space.

Remember that you will be most effective using methods that you believe in, and that your methods can evolve over time. Anything can theoretically be used to anchor your intention to clear a space. Here are some of the most common:

- Prayer or statement of intention: you say what you want to happen
- Color used in any way, as in visualizing the color, placing an object of that color somewhere or coloring an index card and placing it appropriately with intent
- Symbols, either those already known to you, or created/dowsed by you, may be put on index cards or even used as design features with intent
- Fragrance, as in sage wands or essential oils via aromatherapy, again, with intent

- Sound, as in toning, banging a pot with a wooden spoon or playing musical tones with intent
- Crystals may be used to transform energies, to protect against noxious energies or to deflect energies coming into the house when placed with intent
- Pegs of all kinds may be driven into the ground to alter the course of negative lines of energy

You can even use exotic things like numbers, letters, written words or stones with cup markings to effect space clearings.

Just as people misunderstand dowsing, thinking that a pendulum gives you answers, people get confused about space clearing anchors, thinking they are doing the clearing work. Anchors are simply ways to focus your intention. Each type of anchor has its own vibrational frequency, so you need to pick something that will work best with your energy.

It is your intention that clears the space, not the sage wand, not the symbol. Most of us need help in focusing and powering our intention, and physical anchors provide that, but don't make the mistake of thinking the 'magic' is in the anchor. That's why different anchors work for different people, and there is no single method of space clearing that works for everyone on everything. You are the magic!

What About Clearing Machines/Devices?

You will see devices for sale that claim they can clear space or protect you from detrimental energies. Many of these products are simply not effective. Some of them are actually detrimental to your health. Anything that claims to use scalar or zero point energy is (in our opinion) an example of the latter.

A small percentage of products actually work, but the down side is that most of them only work on geopathic energies, or geopathic and some EMFs. None of the devices or products will protect you from conscious sources of energy or cosmic energy.

If you live in an area of geopathic stress, one of the good machines might be worth investing in, but you will still have to clear regularly to transform other energies. Our viewpoint is that if a machine or device doesn't effectively address all types of 'not conscious' noxious energies, it is best to forgo investing in one unless you have lots of disposable income.

What about personal protection devices? As with space clearing machines, some of these actually work. Many do not. None address conscious sources of detrimental energy like entities, curses and alien energies that are active and directed at a person or place. Some supposedly use scalar or zero point energy, and that will actually degrade your health over time in our opinion.

Carefully research any device or machine before buying. If all you see at the website is a lot of testimonials, don't buy the product. If there is no clear explanation of how the product works, do not buy the product. By clear explanation, we do not mean that terms are thrown about without explanation, like 'quantum field' and 'fifth dimension.' Any truly scientific product should be explained very clearly. A product that uses intention anchored by physical elements of design should be handmade, not made in a factory, because we don't know of any way to imbue intention into an inanimate object via a machine.

If you buy a personal protection device after researching, do not combine it with another clearing or protective device. We have shown through muscle testing that doing that can sometimes make you weaker than using nothing.

Devices are a shortcut rather than a good solution to keeping your space clear and harmonized. If you choose to use them, do your research and don't combine devices.

16

AFTER THE CLEARING

A question we often get is how should it feel after a clearing? Is there any way that you can tell, just by how you feel, that the clearing worked? Each person is unique, so it is impossible to give one perfect answer to this question, but the general answer is that some people are sensitive to energies, and some people are not. If you are sensitive to energies, you will definitely feel a shift after a space clearing. If you are oblivious to energies, you may not notice any change.

Can a person learn to sense energies even if they have not previously been able to? Yes. We can't say that everyone who tries will be able to, but if you set your intention to notice and 'feel' changes in energies, it is likely that you will become more attuned to them. Why is this? Your body has a filtering system that decides what you will notice, and what you won't notice. This reticular activating system discards huge amounts of data every day so that you won't be overwhelmed by all the stimuli in the physical realm. If you reprogram yourself by deciding to notice energies in your environment, more than likely, you will begin to notice them. Be patient, as it may not happen overnight.

Slow down and start paying attention to your environment. How does it sound, feel and smell? How do you feel when you are at home? When you are sitting in your favorite chair? Working in the basement? Become more self-aware and note patterns in the behavior of your pets and children. They are wonderful indicators of needing a clearing, because they are so sensitive to energies.

In time, you will be able to tell when a clearing is needed, even if you are not a dowser and can't dowse about it. One client always called us for a clearing when her children started having nightmares. You will learn how to tell when a clearing is needed. You will also learn how to sense that the energies have improved.

Ways To Tell The Energy Has Shifted After A Clearing

- You feel more able to relax, less restless
- The atmosphere feels cleaner and brighter, lighter
- You no longer feel watched
- Areas that were scary become comfortable to be in (children especially see this)
- Unexplained sounds or smells go away
- Nightmares go away (especially for children) and sleep is better
- Visitors ask if you repainted or redecorated when you have not
- Fewer arguments or behavior issues (especially for children and pets)
- Depression and stress seem to lessen
- OCD behavior declines
- You find it easier to concentrate and focus mentally

Will you notice all of these effects? No, it depends on the energies in your home and your own energies.

How long after a clearing before you notice a change? You may notice a change immediately after a clearing, but some stubborn energies may take up to 72 hours to fully clear. If you have noticed no change after 72 hours, it is wise to repeat the clearing if you are not a dowser and can't dowse the effectiveness of what you did. You can't hurt anything by repeating a clearing.

17

STEP-BY-STEP INSTRUCTIONS

Consult your journal for the earlier entry where you noted any symptoms of noxious energy present in the space you want to clear. You can do your first clearing on that location.

Space Clearing Step-by-Step

Step 1: Permission

If the property is not yours, get verbal permission from the owner or caretaker before doing a clearing. If clearing your property or workspace (just for yourself), no permission is needed.

Step 2: Goals

Think about your goals for doing the clearing. Are you doing a regular clearing to foster harmony and well-being, or are you clearing for a particular health or other issue? Be very clear what outcome you are desiring. A clearing may be done for your home, your entire property, your car, your workspace or your business. It is best when starting out to clear one location at a time.

Step 3: Protection

If you are clearing any property other than your home, get protection before tuning in. (Not required for clearing your property.)

Step 4: Tune In To The Energies

Tune in to the property using your intuitive senses to determine the energetic condition. If clearing on site, walk through and make notes of anything you sense that seems to be noxious energy. Make notes of behaviors and events that you are concerned may be due to noxious environmental energy. If clearing long distance, use the sketch or address to help you tune in to the location.

If clearing for someone else, speak to the owner about what you have sensed. Get their input and see if it confirms what you sensed. Ask them about symptoms any resident is experiencing.

If you can dowse, use dowsing to determine what types of noxious energies are present and how strong they are in general, or for individuals. You may use a list or chart of noxious energies when dowsing. Always have 'other' as an option on the list or chart. You have latitude in dowsing. You can go into great detail or just look for energies that are very noxious. Scales are vital when dowsing energies. Below are some sample dowsing questions for space clearing.

On a scale of +10 to -10, with -8 or greater being a serious threat to health and well-being, what is the overall level in effects for me of the environmental energy in my home at this time? (You can ask for another person, which would mean asking the question again for each resident). To get a number (since this is not a yes/no question), you need to select your favorite way of going through the scale to reach the answer. You can use a chart with the numbers and point at each in turn, or just visualize it or say them out loud in sequence until you get a 'yes' response.

On a scale of +10 to -10, are there any individual energies that are -8 or worse present in my home (or on my property, if you wish a broader investigation-- useful if you have livestock) at this time? This question can be altered to include asking for a particular person or animal.

Is the overall energy at my workspace less harmful than -5 for me at this time? You can pick any number you want, but why wait for -8?

Are there any entities present in my home or on my property, or are there any that are usually here, but have left to avoid clearing? This is an example of how you can check for a particular energy. You can also use a list to determine which energies are present. Most dowsing courses teach list and chart dowsing.

Technically, Step 4 is optional, but we recommend it. You can clear without knowing what is there, but you will hone your skill if you take the time to use your senses or dowse to tune in.

Step 5: Choose A Clearing Method

Consult your list of clearing methods and intuitively feel which one or ones will best achieve your goal. If you can dowse, dowse which one to use. A sample dowsing question is: *Which of these methods will be most effective for transforming the environmental energies to beneficial at this location at this time?*

Possible clearing methods (or anchors for your intention) include:

- Statement or prayer of intention
- Color
- Sound
- Fragrance
- Symbol
- Pegging
- Crystal(s)
- Other: if you get this, you will have to tune in and sleuth out what exactly the method is. It might be numbers or something really strange like a certain kind of rock or flower.

Determine how best to use the clearing anchor using your intuition or dowsing. Which method most attracts you? If it's a color, statement, symbol or fragrance, will using it once be adequate? Which crystal is best? (You can consult a book for this if you know what kind of energies are present, or you can dowse a list of crystals).

A symbol can be either one you design or one that already exists. You can place it on an index card out of sight or draw it in the air while making a statement of intention. You can intuit or dowse whether the symbol needs to be in a particular place to work best.

With color, you can color an index card with the proper shade, you can use an object of that color or you can visualize the color filling the space while saying your intention.

Crystals might work best when placed in certain locations. Use dowsing or your intuition to determine placement.

When using fragrance, make sure the residents are not sensitive to whatever fragrance you are using or to smoke if you are smudging. You can use a sage wand or aromatherapy diffuser.

For sound, you can go low tech and beat a pot with a wooden spoon, clap your hands until the sound is clear or use some type of tone or special music with intention.

A good statement of intention that can be used alone and with all the other methods is: *Please transform all the detrimental energies at this location to beneficial for all the beings who live here. Please send all misplaced beings who normally inhabit this location to their right and perfect place in the right and perfect way. Please disempower any curses that are currently having a negative effect on any being or endeavor taking place on this property. Please protect all residents and this property from negative outside influence or intent of any kind.*

Please see the section on Pitfalls that talks about entity clearing mistakes before changing the wording for entity clearing.

Step 6: Do The Clearing

Perform the clearing using whatever method you choose.

Step 7: Confirm Results

Go through the space and get a feel for the energy. How does it compare to before you cleared? If you can dowse, check using dowsing whether the clearing has worked.

If the clearing is for someone else, ask them to note differences over the next 72 hours.

Repeat the clearing if you feel or dowse the energy has not fully cleared. If you cannot get a space to clear, consult a professional you trust. But remember, any clearing is better than no clearing!

18

ON SITE SPACE CLEARING

Start With On Site Clearing

You'll probably begin your space clearing experience by clearing your own residence or workspace. If you are a business owner, you might clear your place of business. This is best done in person, on site. While any method you use in person can be just as effective from a distance, on site clearing allows you to use your physical senses as well as your intuitive ones, and that might help you get more information about the energies present, especially when you are new at this.

∼

Only Working On Site Not The Best For Professionals

If you are a professional, limiting yourself to on site clearing is going to restrict your ability to grow your client base and severely limit your profit margin, as you will have to include time and gas money in your fees. As you will soon discover, the more clients you can serve in a given time period, the better your chances of making a decent living. And the market won't bear the kind of pricing required to support a purely on site clearing business. You will find out that you can only serve a clientele within a certain driving distance of your home for a given price. Still, on site work is an excellent way to build your confidence about doing clearings, and if you're just looking for pin money, it could be just the thing.

Can You Just Skip To The Clearing?

As we mentioned previously, you don't have to find out what energies are present, you can simply do a clearing, whatever feels or dowses best. But, taking your time and doing a thorough job that includes identifying environmental energies will not only yield a better clearing; it will train your intuitive sensing abilities. So we recommend that you do it, even if you feel a bit silly at first and don't trust what you are sensing. That will change.

Procedure For Sensing Energies

When tuning in to energies on site, use all of your intuitive senses. You can start with your strongest one. If you are a very visual person, use your eyes. Soft focus and look around the area, watching for things out of the corner of your eyes. Because you are unique, we can't tell you what exactly your intuitive senses will show you. You may see a gray cloud or what appears to be a figure running. How you perceive energy is unique to you, and we can't say exactly how it will look.

For example, Nigel is very visual and 'sees' noxious energies, while Maggie tends to 'feel' detrimental energies. It impossible to predict how or even if you will perceive them at first. You might not even sense them until you have practiced a bit. And what you sense will depend both on what is there and how such things appear to you. With time, you will be able to interpret what you 'see.' Interpretation is the tricky bit.

Do the same with your olfactory sense and your hearing. An odor that does not belong often indicates noxious energy. One time we had a client report cigarette smoke smell in her bathroom when no one in the family smoked. It went away after the clearing. Sometimes 'house noises' are actually entities. If you are a dowser, you can use dowsing to confirm whether your impression is due to environmental energies.

Set your intention to know what's at work energetically, then tune in your eyes, ears and your nose, as well as your gut. You may not be tied to just one sense. You may have an overall sense of what's what based on how a place makes you feel. You may get dizzy, weak, a stuffiness or pressure in your sinuses, nausea or a headache when you encounter noxious environmental energy. This is where keeping a journal will be helpful for interpreting what you feel.

If a place has a lot of ghosts or entities, you may feel that the place is crowded, even if you are the only one there. Or you may sense a hum of conversations or a strong negative emotion you can't explain. It is true, especially for newbies, that you can more easily sense these things if you are on site. But eventually, you can learn to recognize energies long distance. We'll talk about that in the next section.

Working With Clients Or Friends On Site

If you are clearing your own property, this becomes a fairly simple and straightforward process, but when you are on site at a client's or even a friend's house, how you conduct yourself during the clearing is important for creating trust.

We suggest that you briefly explain the steps you follow during a space clearing with as little jargon as possible. Offer to answer any questions the person has about the process, but request that you be left alone to evaluate the energies. Don't let the homeowner follow you from room to room asking questions and commenting on what you do, as it will be too distracting.

It's probably best to get a clear impression of the energies before prejudicing yourself by talking to the homeowner. Then, after you have taken notes on what you are sensing or dowsing is present, you can share with the resident whatever you feel is appropriate. Often, the homeowner will give you confirmation of what you were sensing.

Don't overwhelm them with too much information, but pick key elements that you feel confident about, or that really stood out, even if you aren't confident. This can be an opportunity to build trust and your own confidence in your intuitive abilities.

When working on site, it is useful to include the homeowner in the final stages of the clearing process, because that allows him or her to set an intention and anchor it. You can have them participate in smudging, hanging the symbol you drew or visualizing a color for a purpose.

Sometimes, a 'fix' needs to be repeated over time if the energy was exceptionally noxious or is ongoing and active, like certain curses or alien energies. So showing the homeowner what to do in person allows them to practice it with your support. It is best to have the homeowner regard space clearing as a reasonable process with logical steps that doesn't require psychic abilities and makes rational sense. You don't want to cloak yourself in ego. You want them to realize that space clearing is a vital but normal process all locations benefit from, and that anyone can learn to do this, but it does require some training and practice.

19

LONG DISTANCE SPACE CLEARING

The concept of clearing space long distance is a difficult one for many people to accept. Don't feel bad if you are one of them. This bias is cultural and relates to the emphasis on the physical and rational in our society. There are many cultures that acknowledge the spiritual and how connected all things are. That viewpoint is necessary when talking about healing or transforming energies over long distances. In reality, it is no more difficult to clear space long distance than it is to talk to someone on the phone long distance.

What If You Don't Believe?

You don't have to work long distance if you don't believe in it. You can still accomplish a lot by clearing your own space and working on site.

It is more empowering if you expand your view of reality to include the invisible, to include things you cannot explain and to allow that maybe some things that seem impossible only seem that way because of your perspective.

A colleague of ours suggests that when you meet a subject you can't get your head around or don't want to accept completely, just 'put it in your back pocket' for future examination. Don't throw it out just because it doesn't appear to make sense now. You are always growing (hopefully), and as you change, your beliefs will change, so rejecting something out of hand does not do you a service if you believe in personal growth.

How Is Long Distance Work Possible?

We can't give you a single explanation, but the generally accepted one is that all things are connected energetically, and that means that if you choose to tune in to an energy or person at some distance, you can do heal or clear energy. Intention is not limited to the here and now, and intention is the basis of the clearing process.

When you use a map to determine your driving route on vacation, the paper and symbols on it represent a far-away location. When you look at the map, you are picturing that other place. You can 'see' features like roads, parks, hospitals. But you aren't there. So how do you see them? You are 'seeing' things via the map. No one scoffs at using a map to 'see' a place that is thousands of miles away. Clearing long distance is a little bit like using a map.

Most methods for working long distance will use a physical anchor to tune into the person or place. Healers who work long distance or animal communicators might ask for a photo, a lock of hair or something connected to the person. This is not required, but it makes it easier for tuning into the right subject. Humans need to learn to surf the energy waves, and mastery takes time, so physical anchors are useful crutches.

For clearing space, a person might provide a sketch of the property. It does not need to be to scale. A sketch is like a map that shows key aspects of the property, like where the house is located on the lot, the shape of the property, the floor plan of the house, etc. We used to ask for a sketch, along with the physical address of the property. It helped us in early days to tune in to the exact property and to visualize it. Later on, we found that just having the address was adequate. A photo linked to an address or a picture off Google Earth would probably also work.

In summary, anything that works for you to allow you to tune in to that object or person or place from a distance is what you want to use. But be open to becoming masterful enough that you don't forever have to follow the steps you did at first.

The actual clearing, as always, takes place because of your focused intention. If you want to clear your beach home or a property you are renting that is not nearby, long distance clearing will work fine. Draw a simple sketch, tune in to the energies and select a clearing method. Carry out the clearing as you would in person. You can place a color or symbol on the sketch, make a statement of intent to clear or hum a tone. The hard part will be getting yourself to accept that it really is that easy to work long distance.

How Intuitive Are You?

When you read this section, do you feel skeptical or afraid that you cannot do this? If so, you either have been programmed to only accept the rational, or you feel weak in terms of intuitive sensing. You can train your intuition, so even if you feel unable, you can still commit to learning to do it. We urge you not to think that just because it seems outlandish, you cannot do it.

If you are very open to doing this, it will probably be easier for you. You may be gifted intuitively or have been brought up in a culture or family that nurtured rather than vilified intuition. It may still take you some time to develop your talents, but you may find it quicker than if you are a purely rational person.

Exercise

This exercise is best performed on a property you are not near and that you do not have an intimate familiarity with. Examples would be if you have a vacation booked at a vacation rental, and you want to clear the space before your arrival, but after the last resident. Or if a family member asks you to clear their workspace, and you've never seen it. If you are familiar with a location, you will find it hard to accept that what you are 'getting' is not just your mind filling in details with what you already suspect or know.

Another option is to use this to energetically 'survey' a location, like a prospective vacation rental or hotel or park to see if it 'feels' good to you. This can be a very valuable exercise to help you determine if you want to invest in spending your precious vacation somewhere. (You have the right to get a feel for an area if you are considering vacationing there.)

Get a sketch, if possible, and the address of the location you intend to practice on. Websites often give enough information for this purpose. Remember, technically you don't actually have to have anything, but at first, these crutches are like training wheels.

Do your protection before tuning in to any location, and don't tune in if you feel you could be harmed by doing so.

It's acceptable ethically to tune in to a property you are considering staying at, and to help a friend or family member with a space they have asked you to clear. Tuning in is in a sense invasive, and you want to limit where you do that and make sure you have permission or a right to do so.

We spent years doing space clearing for clients, and we can attest that if you do this a lot, you will indeed get faster and better at knowing what's going on. Your immediate impressions may be hard to interpret, because the language of intuition is not rational. For example, you might get a sense of the color red if you are visual; you might feel anger if you are empathetic; you might see fire. These could indicate a recent fire, a fire hazard, a great deal of unresolved anger or that they painted the house/room red. So which is the right interpretation? You won't know without feedback from the owner. As you get feedback, you hone your intuitive sensing and get more confident.

Practicing with your intuitive senses can be frustrating, because it isn't linear. But if you stick with it, you will become more intuitive.

Keep a journal of your observations and feelings and see if you can get any kind of confirmation to help you strengthen your abilities.

We suggest if you begin to do long distance clearing for money, that you use as many 'crutches' as possible to assure that you get good results and that you will have confidence in what you do, and then let your methods evolve to be simpler as you gain experience.

20

MAP DOWSING FOR SPACE CLEARING

Dowsers have an advantage in everything, and space clearing is no exception. Map dowsing is a great way of obtaining information from a sketch of a property you want to clear. In this section, we'll just give you the basics about what map dowsing is and how it's done. If you want to learn map dowsing, you'll need to do further study and practice.

This book is not a course in dowsing. For proper training in this valuable skill, see the Resources section for a link to our dowsing course, which goes into the necessary detail to help you master this valuable skill.

Dowsing a sketch allows you to more quickly extract information about the energies present. There are a variety of methods for doing this.

Quartering is used to divide an area into four equal parts. Just draw a vertical line halfway across the sketch and a horizontal line halfway up it. You now have four areas. You can examine each area by either asking dowsing questions like, "Is there any energy in this section that has a -8 or worse effect on any family member?" or "Is there any -8 or worse energy present in this section?" (You can use any number as the cutoff for further examination.) If you get a 'yes,' you can quarter that area and evaluate each section. You can continue to quarter the map to get finer detail about the energies.

We use -8 or worse to indicate very harmful energy that should be cleared as soon as possible. Energy that is -3 might have some mild effects. If energy is -4 to -7, it is moderately noxious and it would be wise to get it cleared, but it isn't as detrimental as -8 or worse. You can pick what number you use in the question depending on your goals.

Another method for map dowsing is to use a ruler that is laid across the sketch at the top or bottom. You can ask if there is any -8 or worse energy present in the area where the top of the ruler crosses the map. If you get a 'yes,' you can take another ruler and lay it perpendicular to the first one and move it along the other ruler, asking to get a 'yes' response when you reach a location of -8 or worse noxious energy. Mark it on the sketch. You continue to move the ruler a short distance, like 1/4 inch, and ask the same question again, marking all locations of those specific noxious energies.

A third way of using the sketch is to have a list of questions about the energies present or their intensity and go from room to room on the floor plan asking them and marking the sketch. You can also use a pendulum, a tiny L-rod or point your finger and dowse without a tool when asking the questions.

If you use map dowsing during space clearing, you can develop your own method for searching for noxious energies. The above are just a starting point.

Exercise

Make a sketch of your property. It does not need to be to scale. Show the shape of your lot, the general location of the house on it, and any structures besides the house, like a barn or shed. It is useful to mark the wellhead if you have a well, because it is good to know if there is noxious energy affecting your water supply. Create a floor plan showing the key rooms, and do a sketch for each level of the house. You don't need to mark furniture, but it can be useful to show where beds are, as you spend a lot of time in your bed, and if there is terribly noxious energy there, you need to know it.

Using what you've learned, find out what noxious energies are present, where they are and how much they are affecting each family member and pet.

Alternatively, make a sketch of your workplace, if you have an assigned work area, like a desk. Evaluate the energies present using one of the above methods or one of your own devising.

Perform a clearing. Go back to the sketch and dowse whether those energies are totally gone or transformed. Sometimes it takes up to 72 hours for energy to clear, so you can dowse whether those energies will still be there after 72 hours.

What You Learned

A sketch is like a map that a person can use to identify environmental energies and their location at a distant place. Map dowsing allows you to perform a clearing just as if you were actually there. You can be as detailed as you like with map dowsing.

21

PITFALLS

There are always pitfalls, but if you know how to avoid them, you can get better results and are less likely to have a bad experience. We aren't saying if you clear space with a sage wand and don't worry about protection and permission that bad things will happen to you. Our point is that you can minimize the chance of ineffectiveness and bad experiences by being aware of the pitfalls that face energy workers in general and space clearers in particular.

Some of the most common pitfalls are:

- Using a method to clear that doesn't get the job done
- Picking up noxious energies because you aren't protected
- Entities vacating an area before the clearing, but coming back after you are done, or entities that attach to a person, animal or object to avoid being cleared
- Getting focused on fear and negativity and being drawn into a cycle of compulsive clearing
- Failing to identify conscious sources of detrimental energy, like active curses and alien experiments, or thinking that one clearing will take care of them

Ineffectiveness

There is always the chance that what you do isn't going to clear all the noxious energies. The best way to avoid that is to be able to dowse well, because that will help you pick the best clearing method and also allow you to check if the clearing has worked. Otherwise, you have to just trust your feelings, and that is less reliable.

Ineffectiveness is often a result of picking the wrong method for the job, but it can also happen to someone who is only looking for certain kinds of energies and misses others. Those who only look for geopathic energy don't find cosmic energies. People looking for ghosts and curses might miss geopathic energies. This is why we've given you a very broad and flexible outlook on the many types of energies you might encounter.

Becoming Toxic

Exposure to noxious energy can be bad for your health. This is more of a risk for those who clear other people's property. If you are only clearing your home, you are not really at risk for this. If you are doing space clearing for friends and family or professionally, you must be more careful about protection and clearing yourself after each project. You can become ill if you do not do that.

Approach Entity Clearing Safely

We have observed that a lot of the people who are attracted to space clearing have a very spiritual outlook, but they still are very dualistic in their approach. They characterize energies as 'dark' or 'light', implying they are inherently good or bad. This is a fairly conventional way of looking at energies, and it can lead to problems. Remember that earlier we said energies are neutral in themselves and can only be characterized as 'good' or 'bad' depending on whom they are affecting. Calling energy detrimental to humans is not a judgment on its inherent nature.

Space clearing should not be a fight. If you call yourself a Lightworker, and you see yourself as a warrior against dark forces, you are setting yourself up for some rough experiences.

What you focus on expands. What you resist, persists. If you choose a dualistic approach to entity clearing, you will often see entities as demonic or evil, while the fact is, most of them have no agenda involving you whatever.

Even those that have an agenda are no more evil than you are. It's just that their actions can be detrimental to you. Characterizing entity clearing by seeing yourself as wearing a white hat and entities as wearing black will attract struggle and danger to you, because some entities are very powerful.

If instead, you approach entities as misplaced beings instead of calling them demons or referring to dark energies as if you are somehow superior by calling yourself a Lightworker, you will get better results and be safer. Think of space clearing as doing housework. You don't think dirt and dust are inherently evil, do you? You don't consider housecleaning a war. You just don't want dirt in your space. Treat entities the same way.

When you clear entities, your goal is not to send them to the Light (whatever that is), but to send them to their right and perfect place. You don't have to know what that is. You just want to acknowledge that there are many kinds of misplaced beings, and they do not all belong in the same place.

If you try to send an entity to the Light, and that is incompatible with the entity, your clearing usually won't work. The entity will resist. If you choose to send them to their right and perfect place, whatever that may be, you are sending them somewhere that is good for them, and the clearing will proceed more easily. Your clearing is a correction of their being misplaced. You are doing them a kindness as well as helping yourself.

ENTITIES NOT CLEARED

Entities are conscious beings, and sometime they are afraid of what will happen to them if they are sent somewhere else. Human entities usually fear being judged and sent to hell. For that reason, entities may flee a property or even attach to a person, pet or object to avoid being 'cleared.' By being aware of this, you can use your intention to send any entities that are normally on the property to their right and perfect place, even if they are not currently there.

Another trick of entities is that they are harder to clear if they are attached to a person, pet, tree or object. It is likely this is because most clearings do not take into account entities attached to people; they just look for free-floating entities.

Dowsing is a good way of finding out if you have cleared all the entities.

THE VORTEX OF FEAR

We have seen people get caught up in clearing energies and end up obsessively clearing and clearing. The awareness of all the many invisible detrimental energies can lead to increased fear and a negative attitude about living on earth.

Like a person who becomes obsessed with germs, you can fall prey to a fearful mindset which leads you to spend hours each day clearing energies just so you can feel safe. If you find yourself falling into this trap, you need to work on releasing fear using a method like tapping or The Emotion Code. We have found the tapping method called EFT (Emotional Freedom Technique) to be very effective.

Certainly there are many things on earth that one can become fearful of, but focusing on fear attracts negative outcomes. Your awareness of energies and how to clear them empowers you and makes you safer. So if you find yourself not feeling empowered and safer, you need to address those feelings and transform them.

Hard-To-Clear Energies

No matter how good you are, at some point you might discover energy that you can't clear, or that is very hard to clear. Don't be afraid to seek help from someone you trust who has experience in this field.

Another difficult situation is when you find active curses or alien experiments or other conscious and active energies, a single clearing might not free you of them. Certain conscious energies can require other clearing work on your part to disempower them, including work on yourself or personal clearing. Manmade EMFs are another example of energies that are ongoing and can be a challenge.

On occasion, ongoing clearing may be required for a time. Usually, the key to disempower active curses is to transform some energy within you that magnetizes the experience. That means you need a healing or energy transformation method to help you get a new outlook and release old ways of thinking.

An example is an active curse from an ex may be anchored to your guilt about breaking up with the jerk. You know it was the best thing for you both, but he heaped guilt on you, and maybe some of his friend or family did, too. You are a suggestible, nice person who seeks approval, and their disapproval makes you feel guilty. You need to release that guilt, as it is the only reason the curse is still affecting you.

In the case of an active alien experiment (some of those cover large areas), you might need to go through a process to show your intention to opt out of the experiment. You have free will, and it doesn't matter if the aliens are powerful advanced beings. You have the right not to be affected by them. A simple statement of intention often works. Sometimes visualizing protection around your property in the form of an energetic dome of blue light or something similar can help anchor your intention to be unaffected.

Most importantly, do not allow yourself to become fearful or angry. Either emotion can potentially put you at risk. There are tigers in the jungle, but the wise human respects rather than fears the tiger, and does not hate the animal for being what it is.

The same thing is true if you have a cell phone tower next to your property or some other EMF source you cannot control. You will need to address not only that energy and its effect, but your own emotional reaction to having that detrimental energy source so close to you.

22

BUILDING CONFIDENCE

Probably the hardest challenge to overcome when you start space clearing is the doubt you will feel about results. Confidence is built through practice and success, so at first, you will naturally feel uncertain about whether you are 'good' at this. Your doubt does not mean you are incompetent. It is a sign that you recognize you are new and have a long way to go for mastery.

Time and practice will help improve your self-confidence. Measure your results as best you can, because that will convince you of success. Before a clearing, choose a number on a scale of 0-10 that represents how peaceful and relaxed and safe you feel at home. If necessary, go room to room and see if that number changes from one place to another. Write those numbers down in your journal. After the clearing is done, wait a day or two and re-evaluate the space for those feelings. The numbers should rise if they were low before the clearing.

Write down symptoms that might be associated with noxious energies before you clear. If your kids are afraid to go into a certain room or they have nightmares, make a note. If you feel restless and can't relax in your favorite chair or find it hard to sleep at night, note that. After the clearing, see if any of those things changes. It may take a few days to be sure.

Watch the behavior of your pets and children. See if they are more tractable and harmonious. How is your relationship with your spouse? Note before and after conditions. If something changes after the clearing, it was probably due to noxious energies.

What if you feel the place isn't quite right, even after the clearing? Do another clearing. Some energies can be challenging to clear. Don't let your ego make you feel like a failure if you have to clear more than once to get it right.

If after a couple clearings, it still feels 'off,' check for active conscious sources of noxious energy like ongoing curses or certain alien energies. Address them specifically by working on yourself and your attitude about them and to protect yourself and remove any magnets that might be reinstating curses.

Not even the most expert space clearer is perfect. Dealing with environmental energies is a journey of discovery and a chance to learn and grow. It isn't just a job to be ticked off your list. No matter how much you do space clearing, there is always going to be a new challenge and the potential of a place you cannot clear, because no one can do everything. But in most cases, you will find that over time, you can become very adept at clearing your own living and working space.

Be patient and enjoy the journey.

23

EFFECTS OF EMOTIONS & BELIEFS

We have seen people become overwhelmed when they first open to their intuitive senses and become aware of the many invisible aspects of their surroundings. The concept of entities, geopathic stress, curses and alien energies can be frightening to a lot of folks. They can't picture themselves as equal to the task of dealing with non terrestrial entities or alien experiments. Even a curse from an ex-lover seems too big to handle.

It is normal to feel a little overwhelmed when your eyes are opened to the vastness of the Universe. If your reaction tends towards wonder, curiosity and excitement, you are a pretty balanced person. Just be sure you exercise appropriate caution. If, on the other hand, you feel threatened, fearful and incompetent, it is time to deal with what is causing you to have that reaction.

If you allow fear, victim energy and powerlessness to persist within you, it is a liability when space clearing. You are going to be tuning in to energies. You will encounter entities, many of which are not very pleasant, though most have no real agenda against you. You will sometimes have to deal with curses that someone has flung at you, or that you picked up through energetic resonance. In order to handle these situations and be healthy and safe, you need to release fear, victim energy and powerlessness.

You might ask, "How am I supposed to deal with alien energies? Aliens are advanced beings!" Or you might say, "How can I be sure that I can help all entities move on, and that they aren't demons who will harm me?" These are good questions. They reflect how your attitudes and energies will affect your approach to environmental factors, and your approach will often dictate not only your success, but your safety.

An example is a colleague of ours, who after learning to dowse and clear space, found himself sitting outside of his house for 45 minutes every evening after returning from a day at work, clearing all the 'demons' and energies he found in his house before he entered. He had a very polarized outlook. He believed he was a "lightworker" and as such, felt there were evil forces that he had a responsibility to deal with, in fact, to vanquish.

We highly recommend that you do not see yourself in this way. He attracted those entities and wasted a lot of time clearing them because of his outlook. Instead of being happier and healthier as a result of learning to dowse and clear space, he got caught up in fighting off energies in ways that sapped his strength and robbed his health as well as his time.

If you find yourself doing space clearings too often or compulsively, you need to work on yourself in terms of your beliefs and emotions. Space clearing is a wonderful and powerful tool that is not compatible with fear or victim energy.

What's The Best Outlook?

In our opinion:

- Don't be judgmental. Don't see energies as good or bad. Remember we said they are good or bad for you, but not inherently good or bad.
- Don't see yourself as a "lightworker" or your role as that of soldier for the forces of good. You are seeking to create harmonious, healthy space, and that is all.

- Don't be fearful of the energies you encounter. Be respectful and cautious. If you find yourself fearful about aliens or entities or curses, do some clearing work on yourself to release fear and learn to tap into your power. In fact, it is wise NOT to embark on space clearing if you have noticeable fear about what you may encounter. That is a sign you have some issues to deal with.
- Don't see yourself as a victim. Victims cannot be victors. You are a victor. You have all the tools you need to deal with whatever comes your way. You are able to evaluate whether you need outside help or not.
- You are powerful. True, you can look at advanced alien civilizations as superior due to technology, but you have free will. You cannot be forced to do anything against your will. You have the right to choose, and therein lies your power. There will always be tigers in the forest, but they do not have to bother you.
- Cultivate peace and harmony within yourself using whatever techniques work for you. Meditation, visualization, Emotional Freedom Technique (EFT), The Emotion Code...there are many methods that will help you achieve peace and harmony. Your vibration will affect your experience during space clearing, and since like attracts like, you are well advised to be as balanced as possible.

24

BELIEFS & VIBRATION

When you are first drawn to space clearing, it seems an advanced concept that invisible energies in your environment can have an affect on your health and well-being. Most people take the conventional approach and act like if they can't see something, it can't exist, or if they don't believe in something, it can't affect them. But you have a viewpoint that empowers you to see your environment in a broader fashion and do something about invisible energies so that you can create harmony and health in your life.

Your viewpoint is enlightened, but it's not necessarily the end. Now that you know about environmental energies and how to deal with them, it's time to examine an even more advanced outlook on environmental energies.

What if everything in your life, everything around you is merely a reflection of your own energies and beliefs? What if you are creating this 'reality' that you move through from your energies and subconscious beliefs?

BLAME VS. RESPONSIBILITY

Most people will be shocked or outraged to hear this. You might ask, "How could it possibly be me that created that noxious energy or curse?" To answer this question, we need to differentiate between blame and responsibility.

Conventional people regard blame and responsibility as the same thing. If someone asks them, "Are you responsible for this?", they immediately assume someone is trying to assign blame.

Blame has no place in space clearing, or in life. Blame is a way of deflecting responsibility or passing judgment. You are never to 'blame' for what is going on in your life. But you are responsible. You have the ability to respond to things, and that is what your power is. Your biggest strength is you get to choose how you respond to what is in your life.

∾

WHAT ENERGY ARE You Vibrating With?

Since like attracts like, your energies play a vital role in your life. If you are depressed, angry, frustrated and upset a lot, then you will attract more of the same. One reason peace and harmony are your friends is that entities are rarely attracted to people who vibrate with positive energies.

The New Age movement places judgment on 'positive' and 'negative' emotions, and we do not agree with that approach. All emotions are valuable to you. They can guide you in how to improve your life. Unpleasant emotions can help you learn to avoid things that make you unhappy or unfulfilled. Pleasant feelings guide you to do things that enhance your life.

There are no 'bad' emotions. But by striving to create harmony and happiness in your life, you will attract more of the same, and that will make space clearing easier and less frequently needed. You can't make yourself happy if you aren't happy. Your vibration is what it is. But by owning it, you can move in the direction of vibrating with whatever energy you choose to vibrate with.

Fear is one of the most counterproductive emotions for creating a happy and healthy environment. If you are afraid, it is wise to use a method to transform and release that fear, because the more fear you have, the harder it will be to create a safe, healthy environment.

What Do You Believe?

Your beliefs have an effect on your environment and your life experience. By beliefs, we mean your subconscious beliefs, which may or may not be in alignment with what you consciously believe or think you believe.

One of the most problematic beliefs for space clearers is the belief that you are powerless. That you cannot change things. That you are incompetent or a victim of beings or organizations that are stronger and more powerful than you. Feeling powerful and able to cope will help you create the life experience you want.

Another issue can be if you believe you have a noxious energy present, even if you are incorrect, it can manifest if you believe strongly enough. Fear will especially fuel such manifestations. We have worked with clients who were terrified of alien energies, and they imagined that aliens were messing with them, even when they were not. Nothing will attract alien energies faster than obsessing about them and fearing them. Nothing will attract entities to your space faster than terror of entities and the feeling that they are more powerful than you are. What you believe can make it so.

A belief that will work in your favor is believing that you always have all the resources you need to deal appropriately with any situation, and that you can learn and grow from the experience.

How Can You Tell?

Look at your life, your home, your working environment, your relationships, your finances, your health. What adjectives describe the patterns in your life at this time? If the majority of adjectives are negative, like painful, mistreated, angry, abused, unhappy, then it's time to look inside yourself and see how you can change those feelings to ones that are more supportive of the life you want to create.

What are your beliefs? Do you feel the world is fundamentally a dangerous place and that you are powerless to change it? Then you might find yourself doing space clearings often, which is less than ideal.

The outer realm is a reflection of your energies and beliefs, so take the time to know what you feel and think, and make changes inside if you want to see outer change. This is harder than it sounds, but well worth the effort, and it will reduce the amount of space clearing you have to do.

Some Examples

If you live in a crummy apartment in a bad neighborhood and have a broken-down car and no money and a crappy job, you are not alone. Most young folks go through a phase of this sort soon after leaving home. This is because once they are responsible for themselves, they often feel not fully equipped to succeed. They may have beliefs or past trauma that convince them the world is a bad place, and they aren't up to the task of creating a happy life. Their inexperience has them fall back on fears and faulty beliefs. But over time, young people learn skills and gain confidence and eventually find it easier (in most cases) to go in the direction they wish to go in.

As a space clearer, you can see environmental circumstances as a reflection of your fears, beliefs and past trauma. If you are living in a space that seems toxic and dangerous, it would be wise to look at your energetic boundaries and strengthen them; to examine your beliefs and emotions and foster positive ones. You are not a bad person if you live in a toxic situation. It's just an opportunity for you to make some changes in yourself and your choices if you want to have a more peaceful and harmonious life.

You might feel that you are pretty solid in terms of boundaries and beliefs, and that you truly are a positive person. Yet you may be living somewhere that seems impossibly toxic. If that is the case, it is possible that you are there to help heal the location. Your knowledge of space clearing could help raise the vibration of the energies there. Don't see yourself as a messiah, but sometimes people do choose to work to improve the energies of a place, and that can be a worthy mission. In that case, it doesn't mean that you are toxic. It means that you are aware of the situation and want to help change it. The trick is to be honest with yourself about whether the surroundings are a reflection of your mission or a reflection of your energy.

Impact On Space Clearing

Since you have an effect on your environment, that will impact how often you need to clear your space. If you are harmonious and at peace, your space will be more likely to be peaceful and harmonious. You won't need to clear as often.

If you are going through a lot of troubles, then you will probably need to clear more frequently. Don't judge or blame yourself. Adding to your stress will only make things worse. Know that you have all the tools you need to create your life experience, and that things can get better over time, and that working on yourself is one of the best ways to accomplish your goals.

25

FENG SHUI

The Oriental art of feng shui is an ancient method for creating harmony in your space. It utilizes various principles for helping to keep the energy flowing well through your living space. While it can be adapted to Western living, it is a complex subject, and most people will need a professional to help them apply feng shui principles to their home, or even to evaluate where problems lie.

Feng shui works to create greater harmony, remove stagnant energy and encourage health and well-being, and there is no harm in applying some of the basic principles in your own living space.

The clearing of clutter is the most commonly cited practice for getting change to occur in your life. Clutter is an outward indication of inner stagnation. If you are a hoarder or live with a hoarder or have allowed clutter to accumulate, you will probably feel less energetic than you would like.

The general rule is to give away anything you haven't used for a very long time. Each object has a purpose, and by giving away things you are not using, you give them a chance to fulfill their purpose, which makes you twice blessed.

By removing items that you are not using, you make room for new things to come into your life that are most suitable for your current needs. Clean out your closets and garage regularly.

Do self-work in order to make these types of changes. Fear is a big issue with hoarders. It's as if having 'stuff' surrounding them makes them feel safe. Also, check your grounding. People who are untethered to the earth will use objects to keep them in the physical realm. Most often, they are ungrounded due to fear. Visualizations can be helpful for improving your grounding, and there are many methods for getting rid of fear, like tapping therapies.

The old stereotype of a housewife rearranging furniture is a modern reflection of the awareness that if you change enough things in your outer environment, you shift the energy, and that often improves your life. A fresh outlook can be very helpful. So by all means, rearrange your furniture not only for appearance and functionality, but to get the energy moving.

Overall, while we admire feng shui and have used it ourselves, we feel that the space clearing techniques in this book are more effective for dealing with modern noxious environmental energies, but it certainly doesn't hurt to add feng shui as well.

26

SUCCESS STORIES

Space clearing works. At the very least, most people experience a noticeable sense of peace and harmony after a clearing. Beyond that, the results can be magical and unpredictable. Here are a few stories from clients we have worked with long distance.

Client Success Stories

Children are especially sensitive to environmental energies. One client always used to call and request a space clearing when her children began to have nightmares. Nightmares are common indicators of entities.

Another client reported that her boys, who normally avoided doing homework and got into tussles with each other, became diligent about completing their schoolwork after a clearing, and they even stopped fighting.

It isn't just kids who calm down after a clearing. A client told us that immediately after we cleared her ranch, a thunderstorm came up, necessitating her getting her horse out of the pasture all alone, which usually resulted in her being kicked. The horse allowed her to put the halter on and lead him out of the pasture calmly in spite of the thunder and lightning. She was amazed, as she had him on a very high-end nutritional program and had energy work done on him, neither of which altered his nasty behavior. The space clearing permanently calmed him. Probably, he had attached entities.

Another client with horses called in a panic, because all 12 of her animals appeared to be colicking. Some were in worse shape than others, but none were eating the hay she put out that morning, and some were lying down and exhibiting classic signs of colic. In this case, we were close by and were able to do a clearing on site. We found that the spot where the hay was stored was being bombarded by very negative star energy. When we cleared the property, all of the horses recovered quickly and began to eat. She subsequently sent the hay out for analysis and was told nothing was wrong with it, confirming the hay was not the issue.

Weeds are a sign of energy that is noxious to humans. We have frequently been told by clients that a big patch of weeds disappeared after a clearing. Yes, went away overnight.

Rats are another pest indicative of noxious energies. We had a client report that he saw a mass of rats in his goose/chicken coop at night. The next day, he ordered a clearing. He did not see any rats after that.

The sudden change in even physical things can be a dramatic result that can't be explained in other ways. Change the energy, and you change a lot of things.

∿

Confirmation Comes In Many Forms

Space clearing works, whether you do it on site or long distance. But long distance clearing can really give you a chance to test your intuitive sensing abilities, because the feedback you get can be amazing. Here are a few examples.

We mentioned earlier that entities can attach to people, pets, trees and objects. When we investigated a client's property, I sensed something attached to a tree, and the entity was very noxious. When I told the client, I had to tell her I couldn't find any other way to describe it but 'demon broccoli.' She laughed and said the tree was shaped like a stalk of broccoli, and it had been giving her the creeps every time she looked at it.

We have observed a pattern of alien energies around human waste, like septic tanks, sewage backups and bathrooms. On one job, we found a line of noxious alien energy along one side of a client's property and told the client we weren't sure what the cause was. She said her husband ran a porta-potty business, and he had quite a few of them lined up in that exact location. That explained it.

In an earlier section, we told you that medicinal herbs prefer to grow in regions with energy that is noxious to humans. To them, it is beneficial. We mentioned a particularly noxious region of energy at the back of a large property one time we were doing a long distance clearing, only to discover that burdock was growing in great numbers there. Burdock is a medicinal herb used for detoxification. Plants can tell you a lot about the energies of a place.

27

SUMMARY

The energy in your environment has an impact on your health and well-being, your relationships and finances. Space clearing allows you to transform energies that are noxious into beneficial energies.

By clearing your space regularly, you can promote good health, peace and prosperity. By using your intuitive senses (and dowsing), you can discover the invisible forces affecting you and harness the power of intention to create positive conditions for living.

You've learned that while space clearing is a powerful tool, the most important thing you can do if you want to create safe personal space is to cultivate harmony within yourself, as your environment is a reflection of your own energy.

The world would be a far better place if everyone performed space clearing on their homes and workspaces.

THE BUSY PERSON'S GUIDE TO GHOSTS, CURSES & ALIENS

BUSY PERSON'S GUIDES, BOOK 3

Copyright © 2018 Maggie & Nigel Percy

ISBN: 978-1-946014-26-9

All rights reserved. No part of this publication may be reproduced, distributed or transmitted in any form or by any means, including photocopying, recording, or other electronic or mechanical methods, without the prior written permission of the publisher, except in the case of brief quotations embodied in critical reviews and certain other noncommercial uses permitted by copyright law. For permission requests, write to the publisher, addressed "Attention: Permissions Coordinator," at the address below.

Sixth Sense Books

150 Buck Run E

Dahlonega, GA 30533

Email address: discoveringdowsing@gmail.com

INTRODUCTION

The Busy Person's Guide To Ghosts, Curses & Aliens, Book 3 in our *Busy Person's Guide* series, covers topics that would raise eyebrows among conventional people. As someone with a B.S. and M.A. in Biology and 14 years working at NASA, I can relate to skepticism, but as I have grown older, I have replaced my youthful rejection of strange ideas with an open-mindedness and curiosity born of the realization that I can never fully understand the workings of this vast Universe. In other words, I now believe that all the knowledge I have accumulated over the years is like a grain of sand on a huge beach, and it behooves me never to reject an idea out of hand.

You may or may not believe in all three of the topics in this guide, but we promise you, the Universe is even stranger and more complex than what is described in this book.

Not everyone perceives entities, curses and aliens as we do, but in our many years of working with clients, we have developed an outlook and methods that have allowed us to deal with them safely, and we are pretty sure this knowledge will be helpful to you.

Our approach is aimed at protecting you from noxious energies associated with ghosts, curses and aliens and teaching you how to transform them. This guide only includes information you need in order to do those things well.

Because our guides are not intended to be comprehensive, we encourage you to pursue further knowledge. About entities, curses and aliens, there is misinformation, disinformation and shifting perspectives and agendas, so use good judgment, ask questions and tune in to your intuition if you take your education further on these intriguing topics.

HOW TO USE THIS GUIDE

We've created *The Busy Person's Guide To Ghosts, Curses & Aliens* to contain all the information you need to become competent in dealing with these unusual phenomena, but you still need to commit to learning the material if you want to master it.

If you can find several hours to dive into the book, you can cover it in one intensive day. We think you'll remember it better and have more fun if you spread out the learning experience over a longer time period.

Most people can complete the book by spending as little as ten minutes a day for less than a month. So break it down into as many small chunks as needed to accommodate your schedule and attention span.

JUST FOLLOW these steps to get the most out of it.

Step 1: Don't skip any parts. There are no unnecessary sections. Each chapter builds on the previous one. If you're really busy, just do one section a day. Commit to doing that until you complete the book. Each section takes on average 10 minutes or less to complete.

Step 2: Do all the exercises. We suggest you get a journal or notebook to write your results in. You don't create competency by memorizing facts. You become masterful by applying what you have learned, by thinking deeply about it. Your participation is a unique aspect of these guides and helps you to learn faster.

Step 3: Get out and practice what you've learned and improve your life.

A Final Reminder:

Don't skip the exercises. Don't skip anything. The goal is not to see how quickly you can finish the guide; the goal is to master all the material in it, because only by doing that can you hope to become competent.

PART I
GHOSTS

1

WHAT ARE THEY?

What most people call ghosts are humans without their physical bodies (dis-carnate). Yet there are many other types of disembodied spirits. In addition to human ghosts, there are animal discarnates and all manner of spiritual beings that never had bodies. Because human ghosts are just one of many types of spirits, we will use the term 'entity' throughout this guide to refer to nonphysical beings.

∼

Types Of Entities

The spiritual realm is unimaginably diverse. In this guide we will talk about the most common entities, their effect on humans and how to deal with them. There are probably many more types of entities than we will mention, but this guide focuses on those you need to know about. Just be aware this list is not exhaustive. Types of entities can be said to fall into these categories:

- Human and animal discarnates
- Non terrestrial beings that once had bodies, but no longer do

- Non terrestrial entities that never had physical bodies
- Nonphysical beings from other dimensions or realities that are so different from us, we can't imagine their form, perceptions or motivations

There is a little overlap in this list. It is designed to help you think beyond the conventional picture of ghosts, which is merely a small fraction of entities.

∾

What To Believe

Some people grow up believing in angels and fairies, and it isn't hard for them to believe in ghosts. Other people were discouraged as children from believing in the invisible. Some fortunate ones grew up in cultures that acknowledged spirits exist.

Count yourself lucky to be open-minded enough to learn about entities, but don't waste time on skeptics and don't take their jeers to heart. We have worked with clients for years and seen the effects of entities, in some cases seeing dramatic reversals in behavior when they were removed from people and animals. This is proof enough for us.

Here's one of the more dramatic stories we have to tell: a woman who had never worked with us previously contacted us, desperate to have us do some work on her niece, who was a junior or senior in high school. Time was of the essence, because the niece was being taken for psychological evaluation within the next two days, and her aunt was sure she was going to be committed to an asylum. Her niece and mother had given permission for us to work on her behalf, so she told us the facts of the case.

The girl was an honor student who suddenly underwent an unexpected change in behavior. For several months, she had said she couldn't sleep at night, because red eyes were watching her. She had on one occasion claimed that someone tried to kidnap her from school, although there was no evidence of that. Her schoolwork had slipped, and she seemed to take no joy in life.

A visit to the doctor included blood and urine tests, and nothing organic was found to be wrong. She had no trace of drugs in her system and claimed not to have taken any. One day, while her family was out, she woke from a fugue state in the kitchen staring at the knife block, with the words, "Your wrists are too bare" ringing in her ears. She knew she was supposed to take a knife and slash her wrists, but instead, she ran next door and asked the neighbor to help her. At this point, her family doctor suggested she be evaluated psychologically.

I could not get permission or enough protection to work on her, so Nigel worked on her alone. It took him a great deal of effort, but he found an attached entity that he was finally able to remove from her and send to its right and perfect place.

The girl was unaware that the work had been done. That night, she slept well for the first time in many months. She awoke the next day, totally back to normal, and the appointment for evaluation was canceled. She went back to being an honor student and sent us a picture of her and her date at the prom later that year.

This story is a rare example of how entity attachment can lead to very negative consequences, but it gives you an idea of how valuable it is to be able to deal with such situations.

What You Have Learned

Entities exist in a wide variety of types beyond human ghosts. Sometimes the effects of entity attachment can be extremely dangerous. Entities can be removed and sent to their right and perfect place.

Exercise

Have you always believed in ghosts? Did you believe as a child and grow out of it, only to come back to believing? What caused you to believe that spiritual beings exist? Write in your journal what your background is on this subject.

Have you ever seen or experienced a ghost? If so, write down about the experience in your journal and note what effect it had on your perceptions of the invisible world overall.

Are you concerned that your friends or family know you believe in ghosts? How do you deal with that?

2

WHY ARE THEY HERE?

There are spiritual beings like devas, fairies and other nature spirits who belong exactly where they are, and in general, they don't tend to have a negative effect on humans, in part because they are in their right and perfect place, an invisible (to us) part of the tapestry of reality.

Entities usually (but not always) are misplaced beings. If something is out of place, it can cause a range of problems from small nuisances to large dangers. Misplaced beings have consciousness, and being out of place causes some of them—those who have emotions—to feel lost, depressed, angry and frustrated. For those who don't experience emotions, being misplaced may simply drive them to seek constantly for 'home.'

When humans die, sometimes they fail to leave the earth plane. Some fear judgment and hell. Others had a traumatic death and are confused about their status. How the other forms of entities come to be misplaced is anyone's guess, but may relate to similar causes, at least for those that are like humans.

Misplaced beings can have a frightening or dangerous effect on you, but the majority have no personal agenda against you. It's best not to regard entities as demons for reasons we will explain later.

WHAT YOU HAVE LEARNED

Ghosts and other entities usually have no agenda against people. Any harm that is done is usually not done intentionally.

3

EFFECTS OF ENTITIES

Like attracts like, so if you are angry, fearful or confused, you will attract things, people and situations with those energies. You will also attract entities with those energies. Misplaced beings generally resonate with these emotions, so they are attracted to those who are experiencing them.

The attraction can lead to an 'attachment' by an entity. The energetic connection usually continues for as long as you resonate closely, until you are cleared of attachments, or until someone comes along who resonates more with the entity than you do, at which point it will jump onto them.

While entities that are free-floating in the environment can influence or affect you, attached entities tend to have stronger effects. An attachment is a more intimate energetic connection and can even become an 'embedding,' which is a stronger link and harder by far to break. Embedded entities will be 'stuck' to a particular organ or location in your body until they are removed.

Here's an interesting story of the case that led me to discover that entities can actually become embedded in a physical body. What's most amazing is that the client was a horse and had no awareness of what I discovered.

I was doing a monthly energy clearing for a client's dressage horse when I discovered an entity that was stuck in the horse's left front hoof. A simple statement of intention did not detach the entity, and when I dowsed in detail (we will mention dowsing in a later section), I found that the best way to describe it was that it was embedded. I worked out a way to remove the entity and send it to its right and perfect place. It was much harder than usual, and I gave a detailed report to the client, who then passed the summary on to the horse's trainer. The trainer exclaimed that that must have been why the horse had been stumbling over her left front hoof. She said the horse would look down at the hoof as if perplexed or offended, and that it had been going on for a while until the day of the clearing, when it stopped altogether.

This was an undeniable confirmation of a clearing done long distance on an animal, with the information being passed through two humans. The client wasn't even aware that the horse had been stumbling. It makes you wonder how often a physical symptom or behavior might be caused by entity attachment.

If an entity becomes attached to you, the energetic connection allows a two-way transfer of energy, which is why you see effects. You can end up feeling what the entity feels. The emotional effects are cumulative, so as you attract more entities, and your energy becomes more angry or confused, you become more attractive to other entities. Embedded entities most often seem to create physical symptoms in those they are attached to.

In summary, an entity can cause physical and emotional effects on the person it is influencing or attached to. Those effects range from mild to serious and in some cases, cumulative.

People who are highly stressed or off balance to some extent will often accumulate entities and become even more off balance.

This highlights the value of regular personal work to create harmony within yourself and also to regularly clear yourself of any attachments. Entities won't be attracted to you as much if you are calm and happy, because you won't resonate with them.

WHAT YOU HAVE LEARNED

Entity attachment can affect your mental, emotional or physical health. The symptoms of entity attachment and influence can mimic other causes, and often, people rationalize their symptoms and fail to get rid of the entity. Whenever you have an unexplained or sudden or excessive symptom or emotion, check for entity attachment or influence. It's relatively easy to clear entities, and sometimes it gives dramatic relief.

4

HOW TO APPROACH ENTITIES

The safest and most effective way to approach entities is with respect and non-judgment. Regard them as misplaced beings you are helping to find their way, and in 99% of cases, things will go smoothly.

Ineffective or dangerous approaches we have seen and do not recommend include immature and ego-driven attitudes that can lead to problems. Treating the situation as if you are in the movie "Ghostbusters" and it's all a big laugh is a cavalier attitude that can get your hurt. Seeing yourself as a "Lightworker" who vanquishes demons or dark forces comes from a dualistic attitude that appeals to ego, but is just as dangerous as not taking entities seriously.

Most entities have no agenda and no allegiances you would recognize, but if you approach them as a tough cop attacking a perp, you can stimulate a dangerous response. Many entities are angry, and it is not wise to attract their anger. Likewise, if it's all a game to you, you will probably end up doing something that opens you to negative consequences. A neutral attitude of respect and with the intent to help them find their right and perfect place works best.

We have observed that it is common when you first open your intuition and start practicing energy clearing, healing and similar methods, that you can end up being swarmed by entities wanting to be cleared, or at least, you may run into them constantly. This is a temporary situation that usually resolves itself over time.

Our theory about why this happens is that there are so many entities and so few who are able to clear them that learning how lights you up like a "Vacancy" sign on a motel. Most people don't have issues during this time. The key is not to feel obligated to clear entities on demand, or you may end up spending a lot of time doing so. Learn to accept you can't clear them all, any more than you can adopt every dog that needs a home. We suggest you use this as a chance to learn to say 'no' and limit clearing to those times you have chosen to do so.

In most cases, entities can be sent on without your communicating with them. The only time you may find it necessary to talk to an entity is if it refuses to move on when you attempt to clear it. Such cases are rare and can usually be resolved by using some simple methods we explain in a later section on special cases.

In general, not communicating directly with entities is your best bet for avoiding conflict and danger.

∽

What You Have Learned

Being respectful and nonjudgmental towards entities keeps you safer and helps you be more successful when doing clearing work. Don't let your ability to deal with entities give you a swelled head, but also, do not feel obliged to constantly be sending misplaced beings to their right and perfect place. This skill does not define you, nor does it oblige you, nor does it make you better than anyone else. It's a great tool to have, and that's it.

5

PROTECTION

It is wise when doing any kind of energy work to use protection so that you are not harmed during the process. Protection is actually second in effectiveness to not having resonance or weaknesses that allow negative energies or forces to affect you. All harm that could befall you relates to your own vibrational energy, but having said that, we all have weaknesses, and it is a good idea to protect yourself so they are not exploited. Since protection is easier to come by than transforming yourself completely, we recommend that as your first step in the process of becoming 'bulletproof.'

When you are clearing entities, your main concern is to avoid having an entity attach to you. Energetic protection can sometimes offset any resonance you may have with the entity, preventing attachment.

Protection can be accomplished using intention (the stated desire not to be influenced, affected or attached by an entity or energy), anchored with something physical, like one or more of the following:

- Statement or prayer of intent
- Crystal
- Symbol

- Tone
- Fragrance
- Talisman
- Helpers (angels, guides, etc.)

The most effective anchor for your protection will usually jump out at you from the list. If you can dowse, use that method to choose your protection and confirm it is a 10 on a scale of 0-10 for protecting you from any detrimental effects during the session.

If you are not a dowser, then you must choose based on what intuitively feels best. Maybe you are knowledgeable about crystals, or you have used angel helpers in the past successfully. If so, you will be able to quickly craft some protection.

An example of what a non-dowser could do for protection is scan the list and get a feel for what will protect you for the job you are doing. If 'crystal' jumps out at you, go online or to your crystal bible and choose a crystal for the job of protecting you. You can focus on your goal—staying safe and protected from attachment or influence during the entire clearing: a 10 on a scale of 0-10. Then you can ask to be shown the right crystal to use. You might just open the book and use the crystal on that page. Or you can take a more rational approach and research what types of crystals work for protection against entities like ghosts. Either way, tune in to the crystal you finally choose and 'feel' if it's right. Then use it in whatever way feels best. Picture the energy of that crystal combining with your intention to be protected, forming a shield around you.

Sometimes during a clearing, you will feel your protection collapse. It is a subtle sensation, but it does indeed feel like a shield has dropped. Immediately stop what you are doing and restore your protection, because failed protection means that there is something noxious present.

If you have no experience using any of the 'anchors' in the above list, you would be wise to do some studying and add at least two of them to your toolkit. While a simple statement of intent can be powerful, if you haven't studied how to power intention, it may not work well for you.

Unless you are sure you can do so, we suggest you not rely on a simple statement as your sole means of protection.

Part of the fun and adventure of learning to do these things is stretching yourself to become more educated and self-sufficient. It takes time to master anything, but with the subjects covered in the *Busy Person's Guides*, you will see a lot of benefits and applications for learning to use intention, intuition and anchors for various purposes. You won't only be using them for protection.

Related to the concept of protection is whether you are safe (up to the task) doing this clearing. In the past, we have on rare occasions found that one or the other of us was not fully protected for a particular clearing job. We are able to discern this by dowsing the level of protection we can achieve on a 0-10 scale. If we can't get a 10 for a job, we don't do it. Usually I was the one who failed to get full protection, and Nigel was able to go ahead alone.

Never do a job if you can't get full protection. Dowsing is the only sure way to know, but follow your gut feelings if you can't dowse. Listen to your intuition. If blocks appear to getting a job done, it may well be your subconscious trying to flag you down and say 'don't do it!'. It is better to turn down a job than to be harmed during a clearing.

EXERCISE

What method of protection resonates the most with you? Try to research online or get a book to help you learn to use it better.

6

HOW TO CLEAR ENTITIES

The vast majority of entities are easily sent to their right and perfect place using a statement of intention. Yes, even though I harped on how most people cannot power intention, this process is usually easily accomplished using a simple statement with focus and intention. This may be so because you are adding your intention to that of the entity, which is already eager to go to its right and perfect place.

Special cases and techniques are covered in a later section for the few situations where you may have challenges clearing entities.

The steps in this section will work in 99% of cases.

Step 1:

Make sure you are protected for this clearing. 10 on a scale of 10 is what we use as a prerequisite for doing a clearing. If you can't get protection, don't do the clearing.

Step 2:

Use a statement of intent to clear the entities. You can use whatever feels best to you, but **do not** send them to the Light (whatever you think that is—most people don't have a clear picture of it). You want to send them to a place that is good for them, not prejudge where you think they belong. Entities come in so many varieties, you can't imagine what their right and perfect place is, so just use that phrase. Here is an example of a clearing statement that works for us in most cases:

For free-floating entities: *Please send any misplaced beings who are currently on this property (or have fled this property or have attached to any person or thing on this property to avoid being cleared) to their right and perfect place in the right and perfect way.*

For attached entities only: *Please remove any entities that are attached to any person, animal or object on this property and send them to their right and perfect place in the right and perfect way.*

For embedded entities: see the special cases section.

Do this with respect and compassion, not fear or judgment. Take a deep breath and release it.

Step 3:

(Optional, but recommended) If you can dowse, ask this:

Are there any entities or misplaced beings currently on this property or attached to anything or anyone on this property?

If you get a yes, you can do another clearing or use dowsing to find out why any remain. If you can't get all of them to move on, check the section on Dangers, Pitfalls and Special Cases to find out ways to remedy the situation.

7

HOW OFTEN TO CLEAR

How often should you clear entities? It depends a lot on where you spend your time. If you don't work and rarely leave your property, you probably won't need a lot of clearing work. Places entities frequent include:

- Bars
- Cemeteries
- Hospitals
- Shopping malls
- Big events
- Prisons
- Schools

Places with a lot of people, intense stress, illness or death will attract entities. If you go to such a place, you risk picking up entities and bringing them home. Your workplace and your children's school are prime places to pick up entities.

Clearing Methods

If you find that entities are coming back home with you or someone in your family, you will want to clear the attachments regularly. One method is to visualize a tunnel of light, white or whatever color feels best, at the entrance to your home, or at whatever door you usually enter through. Envision that tunnel of light removing entities and sending them to their right and perfect place, transforming negative energies and releasing negative emotions. You will need to recharge the visualization to keep it operating. How often depends on your ability to power your intention and the intensity of the energies you are clearing.

A simple statement of intention on arriving home from work, or on behalf of your children as you welcome them home from school also works to get rid of unwanted entities.

You can also set up protection or ask your spiritual helpers to deal with entities that arrive on your property, either attached to someone or free-floating. You will need to refresh that request regularly to make sure they are doing it.

If you cannot dowse, measure your success by how everyone feels and acts and how your space feels. If you can dowse, dowse whether there are any entities present either free-floating or attached to someone.

Exercise

Think about your situation and write down the likely places that you or your family members might pick up entities. What level of stress is in your life at this time? How often do you think you should clear yourself and family members, and what method are you going to try first? Record your answers in your journal, and then revisit them in about a month and make any changes that seem appropriate. Observe how the regular clearings seem to affect harmony, behavior and health. You can assign a number on a scale of 0-10 for how you feel you are doing in each of these topics, or you can dowse the number. If it improves over time, that is a sign of success.

8

"GOOD" GHOSTS

Are there any ghosts or entities you don't want to remove from your space? This book is aimed at dealing with detrimental entities, but there are beneficial ones like angels, guides and nature spirits living around you. Because your intention during a clearing is to send misplaced beings to their right and perfect place, you won't affect beneficial entities who are where they belong.

Most human discarnates do not belong in the earth plane. They are trapped, lost or confused. But on rare occasions, a human ghost chooses to stay in the earth plane as a helper or for a positive reason. This was the case with a client for whom we did space clearings. She requested that we not clear a friendly family ghost who lived with them and had followed them from house to house. They believed he was an ancestor, as he was a pleasant older fellow wearing a stovepipe hat. We assured her we only clear misplaced beings, and he continued to delight them after we did the space clearing.

Beneficial entities and entities who are in their right and perfect place won't be affected by clearings if your intention is only to affect misplaced beings and those with detrimental affects.

9

HOW DOWSING CAN HELP

Dowsing is a way of extending your intelligence, of focusing your intuition and getting answers your brain cannot give you, of getting better results. We urge you to learn this natural skill. A brief introduction to dowsing may be found later in this book. This book is not a course in dowsing. See the Resources for our course in a book.

Here is a brief summary of the ways dowsing can be a big help when you are clearing entities:

- You can use dowsing to discover if there are any misplaced beings free-floating or attached, on your property.
- Dowsing can identify who or what has the attached entity.
- Dowsing can tell you if you have any embedded entities, and where they are embedded.
- When you are devising protection, you can dowse to be assured you picked the best method that will keep you safe during the entire clearing process.
- If you feel odd during a clearing, you can dowse to see if your protection collapsed. This happens rarely, but it is good to know so you can reinstate protection.

- After you finish the clearing, dowsing will tell you whether you succeeded or not.
- If you have a special case with an entity that refuses to be cleared, dowsing is a huge help in finding out what is needed for success.

10

DANGERS, PITFALLS & SPECIAL CASES

Dealing with entities is a serious business. There can be negative consequences if you approach entities the wrong way or get an attachment by a dangerous entity. And there are special cases where the simple clearing method we gave you will not work. In this section, we will discuss in detail dangers, pitfalls and special situations and how to handle them.

∽

VIBRATIONAL RESONANCE

As we mentioned earlier, you are vibrating with a certain energy. If you resonate with the energy of an entity, it is likely that it will attach to you, because like attracts like. Because most entities are vibrating with loss, anger, frustration, confusion, depression, powerlessness and other similar emotions, it is wise for you to cultivate joy and peace within yourself.

You can't vibrate with joy just by willing to. Your resonant frequency is not something you can flick a switch on. The stress of everyday life will sometimes cause you to be angry or sad. You may feel victimized or powerless. When you find yourself feeling these emotions, do something to balance yourself.

Tapping therapies, meditation and The Emotion Code are worth looking into. You need to have tools in your toolkit for transforming energies within you so that you can be balanced when you approach entities. Do not attempt to do entity clearing when you are feeling very negative. That is courting an attachment. Take care of yourself first, then clear entities.

It is unfortunate that most people are unaware of this and do not regularly do self-work to balance and harmonize their energies. There are many reasons why self-work benefits you. Protecting you from entity attachment and influence is just one.

∼

Influence & Attachment Effects

How can you tell if you are being influenced by an entity or if one is attached to you? If you can dowse, just ask if you have any entities attached to or influencing you. But if you cannot dowse, there are signs you can look for.

Remembering that entities usually are resonating with negative emotions, if you find yourself feeling excessively negative, it is possible you have picked up an entity.

If your spouse, children or animals are acting in ways that are not typical, or if they are excessively scared, violent or recalcitrant about doing what they should, it is possible entities are involved.

If you or a member of your family or a pet suffers a sudden, unexplained change in health, it could be due to entity attachment. Clear the person or pet before heading to the doctor.

When there is a room or area of your home you or other family members are afraid of, it can be due to entities. Strange noises can also indicate you have entities present. Nightmares, especially in children, can be a sign of entities.

Symptoms of mental illness can also be due to entities, or if mental illness is present, entities will tend to attach and accumulate. People with mental issues need frequent clearing. Anyone who expresses suicidal thoughts should immediately be cleared of entities, and of course, taken for professional help.

∼

The Danger Of Fighting Dark Forces & Demons

We previously addressed the danger of casting yourself as a superhero who vanquishes dark forces. A dualistic approach, which is often found among those who call themselves Lightworkers, can attract negative entities and put you at risk. There's a reason Superman always has to fight a super villain. If you set yourself up to fight demons, then demons will appear. There is no upside to this, because there will be an endless supply of demons to fight. We urge you not to judge entities and not to fall into ego about your ability to help misplaced beings find their right and perfect place. Try to be grateful you can do this, but don't let it swell your head. And never approach an entity or ghost with anger or a fighting attitude. Some of them can turn your anger back on you and do you damage. Kind of instant karma.

∼

Some Entities Don't Want To Move On

What happens if you do a clearing and the entity won't leave? This is rare, but you need to have tools for dealing with this on the rare occasions it happens. Entities will do a limited number of things to avoid being cleared. They will flee the property and come back after the clearing. They will attach to a person, animal or tree, or even an object, to avoid being cleared, because that bond is stronger and most people don't think to intend to remove attached entities during a clearing of a property. These situations can be addressed by using a detailed statement of intention during the clearing.

On rare occasions, entities will become embedded in a person or animal's body. This type of attachment is the hardest to deal with.

Embedded Entities

Dealing with embedded entities is impossible if you cannot dowse, because only dowsing can determine if a physical symptom is related to an embedded entity. On rare occasions, a symptom is a result of an entity which is embedded in the body.

You can dowse a sketch of the human body or point your finger at yourself and scan down your body to find the location of the embedded entity (you will get a 'yes' response when you point at the location).

If you determine an embedded entity is present, here is a removal method that has worked for us: Visualize yourself holding a sort of big hypodermic (without a needle) which can be used to suck the entity out of the body (much like the one in the movie *The Matrix* which sucked little tracker beings out of a body).

Set your intention to remove the embedded entity quickly, easily, comfortably and safely. Visualize activating your extractor and give it a little time to work, as it tends to take a lot of concentration and focus. When you get a feeling the entity has been sucked out, or you see it pop into the extraction pod, then place the chamber that holds the entity (see it as a detachable segment of the extractor) into a cabinet that will send it to its right and perfect place. Don't remove the entity from the extractor tube. Treat it like it is infectious.

If the entity doesn't appear to get sucked into the extractor, be patient and try again. Remember to be nonjudgmental and have helpful intention for both you and the entity.

What To Do When An Entity Won't Move On

Sometimes a human discarnate or other entity simply won't move on. Dowsing will tell you when this happens. If you cannot dowse, you will have to use outer signs and symptoms, and it will be difficult to trust what you are thinking.

Reasons entities may linger after a clearing include:

- They are afraid of punishment, hell in particular if they are human ghosts
- They have a message for someone and won't leave until it is delivered
- They have the desire to live vicariously by attaching to a human

There are ways to deal with all of these situations, but without dowsing, you are working blind and probably won't gain confidence or have success. We urge you to learn to dowse if you are interested in being competent to deal with situations like these.

Fearful Entities

If an entity won't move on because it is afraid of punishment, just verbally assure it that you are sending it to its right and perfect place, which means by definition that it will be happy there. Usually, once they understand that, they allow you to clear them.

In rare stubborn cases, I have had to use this technique: create a portal that opens on to that being's right and perfect place. Tell it that it can check it out, that you will leave the portal open for ten seconds, and if it doesn't like it, it may come back and you will attempt to find a better place. I count to ten and close the portal. I have never had an entity return. This does depend on your ability to focus your intention.

Entity Has A Message For Someone

In rare cases, a human ghost lingers to tell a loved one something. If you can dowse, or if you can communicate in another way with a ghost, you can get the message and pass it on. Then the ghost will allow you to clear it.

~

Entity Wants To Live Vicariously

We've only seen this once, but surely there are other times this has happened. A human discarnate attached itself to a young person, because it wanted to have the experience of driving a car fast and doing other things young people do. It was causing the human to take risks he normally would not have. When spoken to via dowsing, the ghost said why he wanted to be attached, and when told he could move on and reincarnate as a real human, he was willing to be cleared, because instead of trying to control another being, he could experience life directly that way.

~

Exercise

Keeping a journal of when you do clearings and how you did them and what you notice afterwards will help you to improve your technique and also give you confidence that what you are doing is helpful.

11

SUMMARY

Entities are real, and if they are misplaced beings, they can create detrimental effects on humans and animals. Effects can range from mild to very serious. A statement of intention is usually enough to remove them and send them to their right and perfect place.

Clearing entities is a kindness to them as well as healthful for you. Regular clearings are needed by most people simply because we all go places where entities are present. Doing self-work to help you become harmonious will keep you from attracting entities. Still, some method of energetic protection is advised during clearings. Knowing how to dowse will improve your results and give you greater confidence.

PART II
CURSES

12

WHAT ARE CURSES?

When you think of a curse, you may picture an old hag muttering over a steaming cauldron, adding tail of newt and scratching a hairy mole on her chin. Curses are actually more mundane. Any time anyone wishes something bad for you, that hurls a negative intention your way. How the intention affects you depends on many factors, some of which are easy to control. By the time you finish the curses section of the book, you will know how to identify and disempower curses of all kinds.

∽

EXERCISE

Have you ever wished something bad for another person? Maybe someone betrayed you, and in your anger, you hoped the same would happen to them. Or perhaps you were a little jealous of someone richer, prettier or more popular and wished they didn't have those advantages.

It might be that you are very much in control and stop yourself from doing such things, but everyone has done this at least once in their life, and most people do it rather often without realizing that what they are doing is cursing or sending ill-wish. Have you ever been cut off in traffic and told the other driver to go to hell? Well, that's a curse.

Think about situations when you've been hurt or angry and might have wished someone a negative experience. Make notes in your journal about those events. It is very helpful for you to see curses not only from the point of view of recipient, but also as someone who has the power to curse others. As you know, what you send out comes back to you.

For the next part of the exercise, think about times another person seemed intent on wishing you harm of some kind. Those times may indicate you were cursed. Make a note of the details of those events in your journal, including anything that happened to you after your were 'cursed' than might have been effects of the curse.

Notice how similar a curse looks from both perspectives.

What You Have Learned

A curse is an ill-wish hurled at a person, place or situation. Normal people often send curse energy without realizing it.

13

TYPES OF CURSES

There are many ways you can categorize curses. In this section, we will cover several, because each offers a benefit to you in terms of effectively and safely disempowering curses.

~

Origin

One way to categorize curses is by source. Most curses we've seen (99%+) in many years of working with clients originate with everyday people.

Only a small percent of curses are placed by professionals. Sadly, there are people who are experienced in the use of focused intention who, for a fee, will construct a curse for you on demand. Someone else who would fall in the 'professional' category is a person who is adept at focused intention and uses that skill to curse someone they know, even though they are not selling such services.

Curses by experienced people are harder to disempower and more dangerous to approach. It is a blessing that in years of working with clients, we only encountered professional curses a few times.

A chilling story of such a case is the client who asked our help in disempowering a curse put on her by her ex, who was a voodoo priest. Our dowsing indicated that she was correct in her assumption that he had put a curse on her. I could not get adequate protection to work with her (I suspect few could have).

Nigel was able to get protection, and he found the curse not only very powerful, but it had hidden programs to harm anyone trying to disable it and programs to keep rebuilding it. This is common with professional curses. Nigel was careful to be calm, protected and ready for anything. He knew that as with dangerous entities, when approaching a professional curse, anger can be a real liability, as it can be turned back on you or used to harm you. It was challenging and took more than one session, but Nigel was successful and had no ill effects himself. Thankfully such situations are very rare, because without dowsing, a person who meddles with a highly professional curse is at as great a risk as a bomb squad trying to deactivate a bomb.

If you are a dowser, you will find dowsing useful for tipping you off to the rare professional curse, and it will help you determine if you can protect yourself and safely disempower it. If you are not a dowser and someone comes to you thinking a professional has cursed them, you might be well advised not to take the case. It could be highly dangerous to you.

∼

Who/What Was Cursed & When?

Another way to categorize curses is by the object of the curse or the time of the curse. The only way we know of to determine this is through dowsing. Here are some examples:

- Historical curse (past): placed on a person, place or thing (not you) in the past, somehow now affecting you in present time, e.g., a 100-yr-old curse on the old house you just bought is ruining your finances
- Present curse directed at you by a stranger or someone you know

- Present curse directed at your property, business or some endeavor you have. For example, someone has a grudge against your business and wishes it ill, causing sales to drop
- Present curse directed not at you but at someone/something else that you resonate with, so it also affects you
- Past life curse: this is rare, but a strong past life curse can sometimes reactivate if you are in a situation that resonates with the original curse

Ongoing Or Not?

Curses can also be put into two types based on whether the curse energy is being renewed or not. This is very useful to know, because it is relatively easy to disempower curses that are not renewing—and most are not. The small percent that are being actively renewed are a special case. An example is your ex gets up every morning and wishes you a slow, painful death!

While dowsing is the best way to tell if a curse is ongoing, you can often tell by the details of the situation. In some cases, sensitive people can 'feel' the curse intuitively above and beyond the symptoms of the curse. Since ongoing curses are generally present time and from someone who holds a grudge against you, often you don't need dowsing to identify the source, but dowsing is still a benefit, as it can confirm if you have totally disempowered the curse or protected yourself completely from its effects.

14

EFFECTS OF CURSES

Curses can give you a wide range of effects, from none to illness and death. Most curses are mild, tossed at you in a fit of anger that is either quickly forgotten or replaced with remorse. Rarely will such curses cause serious harm, and they are easy to disempower.

When someone with deep anger focuses on you, intending something very negative, the symptoms will usually reflect the curse energy itself and how it reacts with your energy. If the curse was to weaken or kill you, you will have physical problems. If the curse was to financially harm you, money issues might appear.

A curse that is just general negativity can manifest as anything, but it will always manifest in a way that resonates with your own energy. Literally any symptom can be caused by a curse—any disease or financial issue, even relationship problems. We have seen one case of a very protective dog getting ill and dying from taking on curse energy to protect his owners. This is similar to cases we have seen where dogs protect their owners from noxious environmental energy, making themselves ill. When a curse affects a dog like this, it is usually not directed at the dog, though it is possible that someone can curse your dog or other companion animal, so stay open to that possibility.

How can you tell your symptoms are from a curse? Obviously, dowsing is the most accurate way, but if you can't dowse, answer these two questions:

- How long have you had this symptom?
- Immediately before the symptom appeared, with whom did you have an argument or falling out?

When the curse comes from someone you know, this simple method works well. We have used it with clients for years, and it is surprising how simple observation and intuition can reveal where the curse came from. Dowsing will confirm if your guess is correct.

If the curse is historical or past life in origin, or you picked it up from someone else due to resonance, only dowsing can confirm the source.

You can be sure your symptoms were caused by a curse if they disappear right after the clearing. If symptoms linger, then either the curse is ongoing or professional, or they are not caused by a curse. Once again, dowsing is your best tool if you want details.

What You Have Learned

Most curses are easily disempowered, and any symptoms caused by them will go away. Dowsing is the best tool for dealing with complex or special situations. While the vast majority of curses have mild, temporary effects, professional or ongoing curses can cause health issues, even death, and can cause financial hardship or break up a relationship.

15

PROTECTION

I t is wise to make sure you have adequate protection when trying to clear a curse. The flip side of protection is protecting yourself from curses in general.

∼

DURING A CLEARING

We use a 0-10 scale to measure the level of protection, with 10 being a prerequisite for doing the work. If your protection isn't a 10 during the entire process, you are at risk. Only dowsing can confirm if you have that level of protection, but if you cannot dowse, you can engage your intuition to 'know' how to get adequate protection.

Each job is unique. Don't be afraid to walk away from investigating a curse if you get a bad feeling. Your intuition knows, and it will show you if you don't get carried away by ego.

Being protected is like wearing body armor. You set up an energy layer around you that is impervious to detrimental energy. You use focused intention—being clear about your specific goal—and visualize it in some fashion. Some people put an egg-shaped layer of white or gold light around their bodies. You can anchor your intention with things like a crystal, a symbol or a sound. You can also ask your spiritual helpers to protect you during the session.

We discourage people from using mirrored surfaces as protection, because the intent to send negative energy back to the source is in itself a form of curse. Your intention should be to either exclude the detrimental energy from your life or transform it to beneficial for you.

As always, dowsing will confirm the best method and whether you have protection that is a 10 on a scale of 10. Otherwise, you have to go with your gut feeling.

How To Be Bulletproof To Curses

There is a lot of curse energy out there, and it pays to be like teflon to curse energy. The best way is not in applying protection constantly, although that will help. Your most effective option is to remove energetic 'magnets' that attract or allow curse energy. If your energy resonates with a curse, a back door opens and lets it in to your system. We go into details later on self-work to minimize curse energy.

16

CURSES & FREE WILL

You might ask, "If I have free will, how can curses affect me, because I certainly don't want to be affected." Modern humans scoff at native peoples who believe in voodoo and curses, but modern humans operate under the misconception that your conscious beliefs direct your life experience.

Your conscious beliefs are important, but what your subconscious believes is more crucial, and you can't easily know what goes on in your subconscious (that's the definition of the term, after all). All of us live largely on the subconscious level.

Free will is our birthright, but there are many complicating factors that block it, and most are at the subconscious level. Here are some common subconscious beliefs that block free will:

- I don't have free will (you'd be surprised how common that is)
- I must not exercise free will
- I am not able to exercise free will
- If I exercise free will, I will be punished (or die)
- I must bow to the will of _____(authorities, my religion,

my boss, my spouse, older people, my parents, the government…fill in the blank)

If you can dowse, you can find out which of these you have. Just ask, "Do I subconsciously believe that _____? (insert one of the above beliefs)"

Remember, you don't know what you believe subconsciously. Prepare to be surprised. Many people will have one or more of these active.

If you can't dowse, the only way to tell what you believe is to look around you and at your circumstances and interactions. Do you hesitate to exercise free will if it contradicts what others want? Do you feel that you will be rejected or punished for doing as you wish? Do you feel powerless? Do your life experiences seem to express any of these? If so, you probably have at least one of the above beliefs.

Clearing beliefs can be simple or complex. You can try a statement of intention to transform the energy of the belief, but in many cases, belief clearing is harder than that. It is beyond the scope of this guide to dive into that subject. Just do the best you can to transform the energies if you discover you have any of these beliefs.

Early in our consultation business, a client came to us about a curse. We hadn't at that time had a lot of experience with curses, but our dowsing said he was correct, a curse was the cause of many of his health problems. We were able to discover that the curse was an ongoing one placed by his mother-in-law, and that one of the magnets in his system that allowed it to affect him was the chivalrous subconscious belief that he must accede to the wishes of older women. The older woman in this case wished him dead, so he was in a topsy-turvy situation struggling to survive and still adhere to his beliefs. Because the curse was ongoing, even uncovering this belief was inadequate to totally disempower it. This type of curse is very challenging to deal with, and ongoing self-work removing energetic magnets is your best bet for success.

Self-work and dealing with faulty programming and subconscious beliefs are a vital step in being able to be unaffected by curses. You may be wondering why you should go to all that trouble. Why not rob the curser of the right to curse you? Surely, the curse is a perverted use of free will on her part. However, you must keep in mind that you cannot pick and choose who can exercise free will. All can, or none can. If you seek to limit the free expression of others, you are saying it should be limited for all, including you.

Furthermore, we believe it is unethical to attempt to control the choices of others. Not everyone approves of your life choices, but you would object to them blocking you. In the long run, changing yourself is the best protection against curses. By removing magnets, you block any curse that resonates with that energy. It is far easier to change yourself than to change someone else.

See the Special Cases section for details on how to address difficult curses.

17

HOW TO DISEMPOWER CURSES

It may seem strange that all it takes in most cases to disempower a curse is a statement of intent. The reason it is so easy is that most curses are very weak, and they are in their own way a statement of intent, and you have free will and a right to assert what you want to experience instead.

A simple statement won't usually work on professional-quality curses, and it won't work permanently on ongoing curses. A professional knows how to booby-trap and shore up a curse to prevent easy disempowerment, while an ongoing curse is just the same intent being sent over and over, requiring you to disempower it constantly, which becomes a nuisance. Those are rare special cases.

If you can dowse, you know what kind of curse you're dealing with. If you aren't a dowser, treat the curse as a simple one as long as you can get adequate protection. If the symptom doesn't improve, either it wasn't caused by a curse, or the curse is a special case.

Step 1: Protection

You need protection, especially if you aren't sure what type of curse you are dealing with. By making your protection a 10 on a scale of 0 - 10 for the entire duration of the process, you will help avert negative outcomes. Also, if you cannot get a 10, then it may mean the curse is dangerous for you to address. Do not do a clearing if you don't have full protection.

Dowsing is the best way to tell what level of protection you have, but it is possible to 'feel' your protection drop or change, and if you are intuitive, and you listen to your intuition, you will be warned if you should not try to disempower a curse. This is a vital time to listen to your intuition, as it will guide you.

Step 2: For Dowsers Only

Dowse the details of the curse. Is it simple or professional? Is it ongoing? Is it directed at you? Is it historical? If it's a simple curse, go to Step 3. If it's a professional or ongoing curse, see the section on Special Cases for instructions.

Step 3: Statement Of Intention

Use your own words or a statement like the following to show your intention to disempower the curse.

Please disempower this curse quickly, easily, comfortably and safely and transform any energetic magnets within me and transform any detrimental energy generated by the curse.

Note: Never, ever reflect or send the curse energy back to the one who sent it. This not only creates negative karma and makes you a curser, but if the curse is a professional one, that is one of the most common booby traps we have seen. A professional will anticipate an attack and have your energy sent back to you magnified. So don't do that.

Step 4: Observe Results

Over the next 72 hours, observe any results. If the symptoms have reduced or gone, you are successful. If not, you can repeat the above process step by step. If you cannot see any change, then either the symptoms are not curse-related, or you have a special case, or the symptoms were not caused by a curse.

If you can dowse, you can ask if the curse is now disempowered completely and permanently. You can also dowse if there are currently any curses affecting you. If you get good answers, you are done.

18

THE ROLE OF DOWSING

Dowsing is a skill for focusing your intuition to get answers your brain cannot provide. When you are trying to disempower curses, or even discover if there are any affecting you, dowsing is the best (and only) way. With dowsing, you can:

- Find out if any curses are affecting you at this time, and if so, how many
- Determine what type they are
- Pick the most effective protection
- Find out if it's safe for you to disempower the curse
- Make sure after you do the clearing that it worked
- Uncover magnets within you that allow the curse to affect you
- Find out the best way to deal safely with a professional curse (and if you are up to the task)

You can easily see that without dowsing, you are running blind and at more risk than if you have this tool in your kit. We've written a book on how to dowse if you are interested. It's called *Learn Dowsing: Your Natural Psychic Power*.

19

SPECIAL CASES & TECHNIQUES

There are two types of curses that are difficult to clear: ongoing curses and professional curses. The example we gave of a voodoo curse on his ex was a professional ongoing curse, and though rare, it is the most challenging to disempower.

∞

Professional Curses

Disempowering professional curses is like defusing a bomb. No curse is the same, and it takes real talent and knowhow for you to succeed in disempowering it. Also, it's vital to have adequate protection, because it is dangerous to disempower this type of curse.

When someone is trained in the use of focused intention, they can turn that power to good—healing, or to evil—cursing someone with harm. We believe in the power of intention, but as we mentioned earlier, focused intention is a skill. This is why few people are successful healers, and also why few are effective at powering dangerous curses.

If you can affect others with your intention, it is important to follow a code of ethics. Our code says that it is only ethical to affect someone else with their permission, no matter what your intention, and only to benefit them. Many people have trouble understanding why ethics matter. The subject of curses makes it easy to see why ethical behavior is important.

Trained professionals have the power to do great harm. They learn techniques for rebuilding a curse if someone tries to disempower it. They are adept at hiding curses so that even dowsing can be fooled. Worse yet, they have ways of booby-trapping the curse, so that if someone attempts to clear it, they can be harmed.

The level of harm in a professional curse varies with the intent of the one who ordered it and the power of the professional, as well as their lack of ethics, but in the rare cases we have encountered, professional curses were very dangerous and often had death as the goal. Other professional curses might lead to financial ruin, total career or relationship failure or serious betrayal.

Here are some steps to follow when dealing with a professional curse. It is usually safe to dowse these topics, because you are asking **about** the curse, not attempting to disempower it.

Step 1: Are You Accurate?

It is vital that you be an accurate dowser at times like this. Getting a second opinion from a masterful dowser is a good idea. Don't attempt to dowse about a professional curse if you are not a confident, accurate dowser.

Step 2: Is It Safe?

If you discover a curse and dowse it is a professional one, you must dowse if you will be able to stay protected during the entire clearing procedure at a level of 10 on a scale of 0 - 10. If you cannot, do not attempt to disempower the curse. Be sure your dowsing is trustworthy and get a second opinion if possible.

Step 3: Dowse Details Of The Curse

First, determine if you are being affected by a curse. A sample question is:

Am I currently being affected directly or indirectly by one or more curses?

If you get a 'yes' and are fully protected, then you can dowse some details about the curse that will help you figure out how to disempower it. Like bombs, each curse is unique, so there is no stepwise method guaranteed to work on all curses. This is where you need accurate dowsing, imagination and good intuition.

Some things you can dowse that might lead to useful information are:

- Who ordered the curse and why?
- Will it rebuild if you attempt to disempower it?
- Are there booby traps? If so, what are they?

Who Ordered The Curse?

In 99% of cases, the cursed person suspects or knows who is cursing her. If someone will pay to have a professional curse you, it is someone who carries a large grudge against you, and that person is someone who believes in curses. The person may even have expressed their ill wish verbally towards you on multiple occasions. Dowsing can confirm if your suspicions are true.

Knowing who paid for the curse will narrow the range of likely symptoms. It will help confirm, especially if you are not a dowser, that you are indeed being cursed. Look at the symptoms and compare them to the intent of the person sending the curse. Do those symptoms fulfill the intent? If you can dowse, dowse each symptom and ask on a 0-10 scale, with 0 being no effect, how much of an effect the curse has on that symptom, directly or indirectly. Be prepared to be surprised, as your rational mind often guesses wrong.

Do not make the mistake of sending ill wish to the person you think sent the curse. For one thing, dowsing and the rational mind are not 100% accurate. You may be wrong. Secondly, you put yourself in the position of being no better than they are. It creates negative karma to send curse energy, and it makes you more susceptible to curse energy. The sender will have to deal with their own karma. Take the high ground and refuse to participate in such unethical practices.

Will The Curse Rebuild?

Dowse this: If you attempt to disempower the curse, has it been designed to rebuild? If you get a 'yes', you will need to ask more questions about this before attempting to disempower it, your goal being to find a foolproof and safe way to permanently disempower it. There is no single way to do this. It will depend on your talent, the curse itself and what methods you have to work with. You might find it useful to write down the details of whatever you dowse before attempting to disempower it.

Are There Booby Traps?

Dowse this: Are there any booby traps built into the curse? We define a booby trap as an adverse action that will be triggered by anyone trying to disempower the curse. If you get 'yes', you need to dowse to find out details and determine how you can circumvent the traps in that curse (or even if you can circumvent them). This is another situation where we cannot give you stepwise directions, because each curse is like a bomb, and the details carry the signature of the sender and vary widely. Only dowsing can help you safely avoid booby traps, and even then, remember that dowsing is not 100% accurate.

As long as you are dowsing about the curse, you are probably fairly safe. Once you begin to actually attempt to disempower the curse, adequate protection is vital. Never work on a curse if you cannot get adequate protection, which to us is a 10 on a scale of 10.

Disempower It

Once you believe you have all the details, and you have decided on what you need to do to be protected and disempower the curse, ask if you follow those steps, how successful you will be at permanently disempowering it safely. If you get a 10 on a scale of 10, use the stepwise instructions in Chapter 15, adding in the additional steps you've dowsed are required. Check protection periodically during the process, and quit if it ever drops below a 10.

Get outside help if you feel the need or are not sure of your dowsing or dowse you need it. Do not be ashamed to admit when something is above your skill level.

20

HOW TO MINIMIZE CURSE EFFECTS

There are ways to minimize the effects that curses can have on you, but don't get too excited. There aren't any that are guaranteed, and the most effective ones involve a lot of time and effort. Still, you will be safer and healthier if you choose to do one or all of the following, as they are more effective than not doing anything.

∽

Protection

We mentioned in an earlier section that protection is never 100%. But that doesn't mean you shouldn't use it. That would be like saying that you shouldn't use your seat belt because they don't save people in all crashes.

We regard protection as having two important functions. First, doing regular protection shows your intention to be safe, and intention anchored by action you believe in is powerful. Secondly, protection does improve your ability to dodge the bullets of negative energies like curses. Like a kevlar vest, doing protection is not a guarantee, but it is better than doing nothing.

This is not a guide on protection. We've written a book on protection and pitfalls in dowsing, and there are many good books available on the topic of protection, so we'll just summarize some key points.

Step 1

Focus on what you want to create, not what you fear or don't want to experience. Clearly picture good health, the exercise of your free will and the power to create the life you want. This will help protect you from all detrimental factors. Without a goal or focus, the action you take won't be powerful.

Step 2

Tune in and choose a protective method that resonates with you. Color, symbol, sound, prayer, spiritual helpers, fragrance—whatever you are drawn to. Apply the method however feels or dowses best. Another useful technique is visualizing a protective layer around you that is impermeable to detrimental energies.

Step 3

Renew the protection daily, or as often as needed. Be open to changing the method of protection, as the incoming energies change, and so does your energy. One method won't always work.

Protection is helpful while you do self-work to remove magnets within you and beliefs and emotions that attract negative energies into your experience. This is not to say that you consciously want to experience negative things, but that programming and energies at the subconscious level act as magnets that you are unaware of consciously.

Self-Work

We all have programming, trauma and beliefs from this life and others which affect us negatively. Some of them make sense, while others are laughable. You need a sense of humor when investigating subconscious beliefs.

Healing and harmonizing these energies is a slow process that requires commitment, but it will make you more bulletproof. Some of the most common magnets or energies that allow curses power over you are:

- Guilt or shame
- Obligation
- Victim energy
- Fear
- Powerlessness
- The need for approval
- Unworthiness
- Believing that life is hard and unsafe

Not surprisingly, these energies are rampant among humans. They weaken you in two ways. One way is when you see yourself as a victim and believe life on earth in human form is inherently dangerous, you become prey for predators and a magnet for experiences that will prove you 'right'.

The other way they weaken you is if you feel you don't have as much power or deservingness as another person, or you feel obligated to them or need their approval, you are giving them power over your ability to create the life you want, letting them create it for you, and they won't always choose beneficial things for you. "Allowing" a curse to affect you is the ultimate in giving your power away.

You don't need to be aware of these energies for them to weaken you. In fact, most of us are not consciously aware that we have large amounts of one or more of the above energies. Getting rid of these energies or transforming yourself into the powerful, deserving person you really are will make you less susceptible to curse energy.

If you believe you have free will and deserve to manifest the life you want and that you have the power to make it happen regardless of what others want you to do, many curses will bounce right off you. If you see life on earth as a grand adventure filled with support for you in creating what you desire, curses will slide off you like teflon.

There are infinite healing and harmonizing methods, but no single one does it all. We have studied and mastered many: SRT (Spiritual Response Therapy), EFT (Emotional Freedom Technique), Senzar Clearing. We have also practiced the use of symbols, color, fragrance, toning, The Emotion Code and other methods.

We aren't going to say you need to learn this or that method, because you are unique. What works for us might not work for you. Have clear goals and ask to be shown what will most help you. The answer will present itself. Jump on it, or if you feel reservations because it's expensive or seems challenging in other ways, refine your goals and ask again for a solution that meets all your criteria.

Many people invest lots of time and money in things that don't work for them, but may work for others. Use your intuition before diving in, but once you get a clear sign, don't hesitate to take action.

It is wise to have more than one tool in your kit for obvious reasons. Different problems require different solutions. We suggest you become expert with at least two methods. More is better.

Be patient on your journey of healing and transformation. Measure success not over days, but over months and years.

Release Judgment & Duality

We live in a dualistic world. Good and bad, up and down, black and white. The duality allows us to form preferences. Without the duality, there would be no choice. With duality, however, we tend to form judgments that say our preference is good and others are bad. This leads to conflicts of all sizes, and curses are one form of energy that comes from making judgments against others and their choices.

Fear and anger at the choices others make can lead to hurling ill wish energy at them or them at you. Do your best never to yield to that temptation, because if you curse others, you will attract curse energy yourself.

People will disagree with you no matter how good a person you are, no matter how hard you try to make 'good' choices, because we all see things from different perspectives. We live in a free will Universe, and it's helpful to let go of trying to win approval or make judgments, as those actions come from fear of retribution or fear of different viewpoints.

One of the most useful attitudes you can have when doing self-work is to choose to do your best and get on with your life and allow others to get on with theirs. Allow others the free will to think of you as they wish, and don't feel a need to change their mind about you.

The world will always have contrast and variety in the form of different beliefs and behaviors. You are not here to change the world. You can try if you wish, but if that is your goal, do it not by fighting others who are different, not by trying to convert others, but by living what you believe and being a good example of peace, love and harmony.

What you focus on expands, and what you resist persists. Don't ever give energy to what you don't want. Release judgment of those who are different. Don't give them your power by fearing them or being angry with them—that opens the door to curses. They can be insignificant in your life or powerful. You have the freedom to choose the perception you wish, and that choice will affect your life experience. You are that powerful.

Exercise

In your journal, describe what methods of protection you use or have used in the past. How has your protection evolved over time? If you are new to this topic, explore the many options you have and record in your journal which ones most appeal to you, and why you think that is.

What subjects are you most judgmental about? How could those subjects relate to fear on your part? What would eliminating fear do to your perception of the challenges?

To whom or what have you formed a pattern of giving your power to in the past? Do you seek approval from family or spouse? Do you do things to get your boss to recognize your value? Do you feel less valuable because you don't have letters after your name?

What methods are you capable of using for self-growth? If you are already using one or more methods, what type of changes have you seen over time through using them? Have you abandoned certain methods for others, and why do you think that is so?

If you are new to self-work, what methods most attract you? Try to commit to learning at least two methods and then use them regularly. Record your results in your journal.

21

SUMMARY

Ill wish is a fact of human life. In most cases, curses are weak and temporary in their effect. A simple statement of intention will disempower them.

In rare cases, the one who sent the curse was powerful or trained in the use of intention, or they keep sending the curse energy, and disempowering such curses can be difficult or even dangerous.

Protection is vital when working with curses, but self-work to align with your own power is even better, although it takes time to do that. We recommend you learn a few transformational methods and practice them regularly to help remove the energetic 'magnets' that allow curses to affect you. Theoretically, you can become bulletproof to curses if you work at it.

Curses exist, but to blame everything that's wrong in your life on curses and not work on yourself to prevent them is to be a victim. Taking responsibility for your life experience is stepping into your power and will tremendously improve your life.

Dowsing is a tremendous tool in dealing with curses, especially special cases. We would not be without dowsing when working on curses.

PART III
ALIENS

PART III

ATHENS

22

WHAT ARE ALIENS?

Historical Perspective

There are many references in human history to alien visitation of Earth and even to aliens tampering with Earth's flora and fauna, especially humans. A search on the internet will yield descriptions of many incidents, some dating back to ancient India and the Middle Ages in Britain, where humans reported seeing flying vehicles making war or crashing or just creating a symphony of flashing lights in the sky. In recent history, there is the story of the Roswell crash, poorly explained as a malfunctioning weather balloon. Reports of cattle mutilation, alien abduction and strange lights in the night sky appear over the last several decades at locations all around the world.

Perhaps the person who most investigated and wrote about ancient alien visitation was Zechariah Sitchin, who wrote a series explaining the rise of Sumerian civilization as an alien artifact which included genetic modification of ancient humans to make modern Homo sapiens. His interpretations have stirred up controversy as have other authors on related topics. Regardless of one's opinions, it is a fact that there are many reliable sources who have seen or believe in alien life forms, including NASA astronauts. The unanswered question is why do they visit Earth, and we believe there are many different and accurate answers to that question, in fact, as many answers as there are species of aliens visiting this planet. It's not part of the scope of this guide to pursue these topics in depth, but there are many resources online and in books if you are interested.

∼

What Are Aliens To You?

Let's bypass the question of whether aliens exist, because it's one of those topics that no matter what evidence you present, most people have already made up their minds. You're probably not a skeptic, or you wouldn't be reading this book. At the very least, you are open-minded. So, instead of wasting time trying to prove aliens exist, let's dive into what you need to know so you can deal with aliens and alien energies.

An alien is a being who is not of Earth. Probably 99.9% of aliens haven't even heard of Earth, so the ones we will discuss are the few who meddle in Terran affairs for whatever reason.

Think about what this fact means. Contrary to movies and sci-fi stories which center around how aliens affect humans, most aliens have no more interest in humans than humans have in earwigs. This is good news. It means aliens in general are not automatically something to fear. On the other hand, it would be unwise to assume all aliens are harmless. If they were, you wouldn't need this guide.

This guide will help you deal with those rare aliens that meddle with Earth affairs, especially human life, either in person or at a distance, or whose actions on Earth have a negative effect on humans.

What are the chances that you will encounter an alien in person? Unlikely. In nearly 20 years of working with clients and talking to people at events, we have heard of only a few who have spotted aliens, and even in those cases, there was no obvious ill intent on the part of the aliens. This is not to minimize the cases where aliens do have ill intent, but to help you put things in perspective.

The bottom line is that even though aliens exist, you're not likely to ever meet one, but on occasion, you might be affected by alien energies of some kind. This guide will give you tools for handling the most common types safely and effectively.

The Good News

The good news is that of the three types of energies in this book, alien energies are the rarest. You might not even run into them. This section of the guide will give you tools for dealing with them if you do.

Exercise

In your journal, describe how you view aliens in general. Has that perspective evolved over time? What has influenced your attitude?

Have you or anyone you know had an encounter or viewing of an alien or alien vehicle? What was it like? How has that event affected your viewpoint on aliens?

23

TYPES OF ALIEN ENERGIES

Types Of Aliens

Good vs. Bad

The most useful way to categorize aliens is by their effect on humans. The small percentage of aliens who know about humans and actively interact with them fall into one of two categories: beneficial or detrimental to humans.

This book isn't about describing all alien species. There are plenty of sources, reliable and not, for that information. We also won't spend any time on beneficial aliens, as they are helpful, not harmful. We aren't even concerned with identifying species of detrimental aliens, because our main goal is to help you avoid the effects of noxious alien energies, not necessarily knowing which aliens are which.

Just know that there are multiple species of 'bad' aliens, but you don't need to identify which species you are dealing with in order to neutralize a threat.

Past Or Present

Another way to categorize aliens is by whether they are affecting humans now or through past events that carry strong alien energies. Historical alien energies can represent ancient wars or slaughter conducted by aliens at some location on earth (the Middle East is a good example of this), and those energies can be just as powerful as present time alien energies.

In Person Or At A Distance

Another way to type aliens is by whether they are acting in person on earth or from far away.

Focused On You Or Not

Finally, you could type alien energies by whether they are directed at you specifically (this is rare), or if they are affecting a large area or big population of humans.

Of course, there is overlap in these systems, so you could have, for example, an alien experiment currently active that is targeting people who live in a certain city and is being directed from another planet.

24

ARE ALL ALIENS BAD?

As mentioned earlier, aliens are like energy in general. Some have a negative effect on humans, and some have a positive effect. They are not inherently good or evil. Most aliens aren't even aware of the tiny planet called Earth on the edge of the Milky Way galaxy, and maybe this is a good thing. As a fellow NASA researcher once asked about SETI (Search for Extraterrestrial Intelligence), "Why is everyone assuming it would be a good thing to let aliens know we're here?"

People seem to be divided into two camps about aliens. There are the "ET" ones, who picture aliens as benevolent space travelers who are less harmful to us than we are to them. And then there are the "X Files" ones, who imagine aliens as wanting to use us or put tracking devices in our heads. The reality is probably both. Some aliens would be like ET, and others want to mine Earth and use humans for various selfish purposes.

If you are going to deal with alien energies, the safest attitude is to be aware that aliens are not all good or all bad. Even the ones who have detrimental effects on humans are mostly no worse than scientists who raise lab rats and use them in experiments that end in their suffering or death (the rats, not the scientists). To many aliens, we are no better than lab rats. When you step on a cockroach or ignore animal experimentation, saying it's for a good cause, remember that you are an insect or lab rat to some aliens.

Alien energies can have a dreadful effect on humans, but it is important not to fear aliens. Fear will not help you overcome the challenges of alien energies. In fact, it will attract them.

This guide is meant to empower you to be safe even if you find there are alien energies in your environment. Be cautious, be smart and be empowered.

WHAT YOU HAVE LEARNED

Aliens come in many varieties, and some have detrimental effects on humans, but it will only harm you to fear aliens. We have seen people who, once they accept that aliens exist and that some are detrimental, become terribly afraid. Don't go this route. You can choose to be empowered to deal with alien energies and live safely and without interference. You have free will, and you have the right not to be messed with by anyone, including aliens.

25

EFFECTS OF ALIEN ENERGIES

If you have read this entire guide, you will begin to see some similarities in the effects on you of ghosts, curses and aliens. There are at least two reasons that these very different sources can have similar effects. First, unlike most noxious energies in your environment, the energies of ghosts, curses and aliens can have a conscious element, that is, intention and activity that regenerates the energies. Secondly, your reaction to any noxious energies will be in part determined by your own energies and beliefs, which can lend a similarity to the patterns of effects you see.

Detrimental alien energies can harm your health, your finances, your relationships and your business, if you have one. The intensity of the effects can range from mild to very serious. As we have pointed out before, if you cannot dowse, then the only way you can know whether a symptom is due to alien energies is if, after the clearing, the symptom reduces or goes away completely.

Most alien energies can be dealt with effectively. After years of working with clients all over the world, we have found that alien energies are more concentrated and detrimental in certain locations. That may be due to historic or current alien activity, or both.

At the time of this writing, particular areas where we noticed alien energies in the US are the Pacific Northwest, the DC area and parts of Texas and Florida. There is alien energy in other parts of the US as well, but those are where we repeatedly saw alien energies when working with clients.

Outside of the US, the Middle East is particularly affected by alien energies. Parts of Portugal, South Africa and Australia were likewise affected. Of course, our data is limited to where we worked long distance with clients to do space clearings, so there could be other areas equally affected.

There doesn't seem to be a correlation between population density and alien energies. Some affected areas were very rural and undeveloped, while others had long histories of human residence. We do believe, however, that major seats of government are more likely to have alien energies, based on the intensity of energies around the US capital city.

Since alien energies are a type of environmental energy, if you have recently moved to a new location or begun work at a new job, it is possible that new symptoms are caused by alien energies (or some other environmental energy). However, even if you have lived someplace for a long time, a new symptom can possibly be due to new alien energies affecting that location.

If you live in an area that has lots of alien energies, just as if you live in other toxic environments, it will take more work to keep your space healthy and harmonious.

You'll get tired of us saying this, but the only way to be sure what's going on is to be a good dowser. Dowsing will help you identify the source of energies and how best to deal with them. Without dowsing, you can use the protocol in this guide to clear alien energies, but you will be operating in partial blindness. Be sure to read and apply the advice on protection.

Just about any symptom you are experiencing can be caused by alien energies, but like curses and entities, alien energies are not as common as other types of noxious energies, so don't assume anything.

Levels Of Effects

To simplify a complex topic, you can regard alien energies as falling into one of the following categories with common levels of intensity or effects:

- Historical alien energies can be mild to serious, but will not regenerate and are not directed at anyone
- Active alien influence or interference can be mild to serious, but usually is mild and fairly easy to clear. It may be directed at an individual or a group or location by a single alien or group of aliens, but isn't part of an organized program or project. We use the words 'influence' and 'interference' to indicate a level of activity that has an effect, but generally does not have a long term goal that causes great harm to humans.
- Active alien experimentation is very rare, and it is usually moderate to serious and can cover a large area. This type of energy seems to require more care to clear and more protection to keep you safe. Humans in this case may be used as lab rats, or there may be a goal of having a particular outcome in human society. We have only seen experiments that cover groups of humans (as opposed to individuals), and that allows you to opt out unnoticed and be unaffected.
- Alien abduction or alien implants are actual physical interference with humans. These are rare situations and beyond the scope of this book, which focuses on energetic effects. Fortunately, such actions appear to be very rare, and you are unlikely to encounter them. As with all things, your energy is the most important contributing factor to what you experience.

You do not need to identify the alien energies before clearing them, but if you are a dowser, finding out which type of energy will give you a clearer idea of how serious it is and how best to safely approach it.

What You Have Learned

It can be challenging to determine if your symptom is caused by alien energies unless you can dowse accurately. Alien energies are not as common as many other detrimental energies and don't have specific markers. They are a type of environmental energy that, like curses and entities, have a conscious component, because the energy originates from a being. Without dowsing, there is no sure way to know that alien energies are your problem, but the good news is that you can use the methods in this guide to clear alien energies effectively in the vast majority of cases even if you are not a dowser.

26

PROTECTION

No matter what energy you are clearing, protection is a very good idea. What we have said in the previous sections on protection applies to alien energies. Any type of energy can accidentally be 'picked up' by you, and conscious energies are probably the most risky that way, as they can be programmed to affect you. There are infinite methods of protecting yourself, and you can even use the ones described in the earlier sections, because the goal of protection is always the same: to protect you from the detrimental effects of noxious energies.

If you cannot dowse, and most people cannot, then when you are working with alien energies, you are working blind. That means it is probably wise to assume from the start that you are dealing with a dangerous energy, whether it is or not. Better safe than sorry.

You can't overdo protection, so it makes sense to be excessively cautious rather than reckless. Of the three energies we discuss in this book, alien energies in our experience are the most challenging of these three very unusual energies. We pointed out that there are very dangerous entities, and that is true, but they are very rare. Curses can also kill a person, but a professionally done curse is also exceedingly rare. Alien energies are not that common, and the worst ones are indeed rare, but in our experience, they are more common than bad curses and horrible entities.

It doesn't really matter if that is true, though. The important thing is that you take proper precautions when clearing alien energies. This is a stepwise description of how to protect yourself even if you cannot dowse, as it assumes you don't know exactly what type of alien energy you are dealing with or how noxious it is. It assumes the worst, so as to keep you safe. (Dowsers can use the additional steps listed.)

Step 1: Evaluate & Prepare

Assume you are dealing with active, noxious alien energies that represent an experiment with very noxious effects. Tune in to your emotions. If you have any feelings of fear, do not proceed until you transform or clear them using your favorite method. We like tapping or toning. As long as you are feeling any fear, you are at risk, so if you cannot feel strong, do not attempt a clearing.

Dowsers: dowse if your symptom is caused by alien energy, or if there is alien energy in your space, and if so, how strongly it is affecting you on a scale of 0-10.

If you are feeling strong, then affirm your right to choose your life experience. You have free will, and you have the right NOT to be affected by anyone else's choices, even those of aliens. If this feels like a weak affirmation, do self-work until it is strong, and do not proceed with the clearing if it feels weak.

Step 2: Choose Protection

Select whatever form of protection is your favorite and feels best for the goal of keeping you 100% protected during the entire clearing process. Your goal is to stay hidden from aliens and any surveillance they have and to stay 100% protected from noxious energies and programs.

You can use anything that works for you. We have found sometimes that a layer of blue light surrounding you completely is a good method. However, you may use sound, crystals, symbols, color, an amulet, spiritual helpers or a combination of any of these things. Allow your intuition to guide you.

Dowsers: dowse if there is a method that will give you 100% protection for the duration of the clearing. If not, don't do the clearing. If so, dowse what the method is and how to apply it.

Step 3: Evaluate Your Protection

Tune in and see how safe you feel after applying the protection. If you have anything less than 100% confidence, do not proceed with the clearing. If your protection feels 100%, then proceed with the clearing process according to the steps listed in that section.

Dowsers: dowse what level of protection you have once you have applied it.

Go on to Chapter 28 to do the clearing.

27

THE ROLE OF DOWSING

Dowsing is a way to expand your ability to gather facts about the invisible forces that you are attempting to deal with. Your rational mind is unable to give you the details about the energies you want to clear. Your brain may guess there is alien energy, but it's simply a guess. Without accurate dowsing, you just can't be sure.

Likewise, when you choose protection or a method for clearing the alien energies, if you cannot dowse, you will have to simply tune in and let your intuition guide you. Intuition is wonderful, but being able to focus it with dowsing is far more powerful. Your chances of success and being safe are dramatically improved if you are a good dowser.

Once the clearing is done, dowsing will allow you to confirm how successful it was. The peace of mind this gives you is priceless.

Dowsing is useless to you if you are not an accurate dowser. See the Resources for our course in a book if you are interested in adding this tool to your toolkit.

When dealing with invisible energies like aliens, dowsing is like having a superpower. It will give you confidence, help keep you safe and assure you of greater success.

In summary, with dowsing you can do the following things that you cannot do without it:

- You can identify and confirm that an energy affecting you is alien or not
- You can determine the level in effects of that energy on you and the general type of energy it is
- You can find the best method of protection or if it is not safe for you to attempt to clear the energy
- Dowsing will help you choose the most effective clearing method
- You can confirm that the clearing has worked
- You can use dowsing to check in from time to time and find out if any alien energy is affecting you

28

HOW TO CLEAR ALIEN ENERGIES

The effects of non terrestrial beings on you can be minimized or blocked or cleared in most cases. Remember that this clearing procedure will not affect any beings who are helping you ethically. Your angels and guides will not be harmed or blocked by doing a clearing, because your intention is focused on transforming energies that are detrimental and blocking those energies that would interfere with your free will and well-being.

You don't have to be psychic and know all the details of the alien energies that are affecting you in order to clear them, but as we've said repeatedly, dowsing will give you an advantage by helping you be sure what you are dealing with and that your clearing process succeeded. If you are not a dowser, you can still follow this protocol and in most cases successfully deal with alien energies.

In this stepwise procedure, we will include extra steps for dowsers, but if you cannot dowse, just skip those parts.

Step 1: Protection

You need protection, especially if you aren't sure what type of alien energy you are dealing with. By making your protection a 10 on a scale of 10 for the entire duration of the process, you will help avert negative outcomes. Also, if you cannot get a 10, then it may mean the energy is dangerous for you to address.

Do not do a clearing if you don't have full protection. Dowsing is the best way to tell what level of protection you have, but it is possible to 'feel' your protection drop or change, and if you are intuitive, and you listen to your intuition, you will be warned if you should not try to disempower a certain alien energy. This is a vital time to listen to your intuition, as it will guide you.

Step 2: For Dowsers Only

Dowse the details of the alien energy. Dowse if it will respond well to a normal clearing procedure, meaning will it succeed and be safe for you. If you get 'yes', go to Step 3. If you get 'no', read the section on Special Cases for ideas and dowse if it is simply something you shouldn't mess with, or if you need special protection or outside help or to do a special clearing like a visualization.

Step 3: Statement Of Intention With Or Without An Anchor

Use your own words or a statement like the following to show your intention. You may add an 'anchor' of some sort, like a crystal, symbol, color or even assistance from your spiritual helpers to make it more effective. We have found that visualizing a dome of electric blue light over your property and refreshing it periodically can be protective in many cases.

Please transform any alien energies currently affecting me, my property or my family to beneficial and set up protection to block further interference if the energy is an active one. I choose to opt out of any alien experiments that are affecting me, quickly, safely, permanently and comfortably.

Step 4: Observe Results

Over the next 72 hours, observe any results. If the symptoms you suspect or dowsed are due to alien energies have reduced or gone, you are successful. If not, you can repeat the above process step by step. Try to vary the statement and anchor. If you cannot see any change, then either the symptoms are not related to alien energies, or you have a special case.

If you can dowse, you can ask if the alien energy is now gone completely and permanently. You can also dowse if there are currently any alien energies affecting you. If you get good answers, you are done.

29

SPECIAL CASES

Some alien energies are tough to deal with. Others are dangerous to deal with, or at least, it's important to act with caution, just as with entities. Also, we've noticed that certain items and usage seem to attract alien energies. In this section, we will address some of the rare cases that we have come upon that have been atypical and had pitfalls of some kind, and we will share with you where we often have seen alien energies.

∽

Places We've Found Alien Energies Repeatedly

We have done a lot of space clearings for clients around the world, and what we noticed was that alien energies seem to gravitate to certain types of things or functions. We often found alien energies associated with septic systems, septic fields and bathrooms. Anything to do with excrement. One notable instance was a long distance clearing in a Western rural area on acreage, where we found a linear area of concentrated alien energies just inside and along the property line. When we reported it to the owner, she commented that her husband ran a porta potty business, and that's where he stored his portable toilets, and that he had a row of them in that location. This was clear confirmation of that association, as we had no prior knowledge of this.

Another place we have often found alien energies is associated with wiring and routers of computers. Maybe anything that is advanced technology would be more energetically attractive to aliens or their energy.

This does not indicate aliens are targeting your bathroom or computer. It's just that like attracts like, and for some reason we have seen more alien energies associated with these two situations than any other.

~

CAN'T Clear The Energy

In all our years of working with clients, we only had one case where repeatedly clearings did not transform the alien energies present on the property. The location was a sparsely populated ranch in the northwestern US, and it had suffered a number of unpleasant events that we traced to historical alien energies. Keep in mind that this is very rare, and you are unlikely to ever run into this sort of thing.

On this ranch, the owners had a large herd of elk they were raising for market. When a blood test detected a certain disease was present in one of the elk, the health department ordered the owners to put all the elk down. Later, when appealing the decision, after the elk had all been destroyed, it was revealed to the owners that no one associated with the Health Department was able to find the original test results. The owners were not only financially devastated, but emotionally very disturbed by this event, because they believed that it was possible the single test done had been inaccurate.

During a dowsing session, we found powerful alien energy present on the property that had to do with a slaughter many years ago. What happened to the elk was a manifestation of the 'slaughter' energy. We did our best to clear this historical energy. A short while later, a herd of sheep that were a very expensive breed they were raising were all killed in broad daylight by a mountain lion that went over a 10 ft fenced enclosure near the house during a party. All the sheep were killed; the lion didn't even try to eat them. We continued to do clearings on the property, varying our methods, but the alien energies remained.

They had told us they had seen UFO-type lights at night, and they were not flighty people, so there appeared to also be active energies at work there.

The clearings we performed were done at a distance, and most clearings work fine that way, but in this case, we felt that unless we went there in person, we weren't going to totally succeed. The owners chose to put the property for sale instead, because this particular energy was manifesting as death on a large scale, in addition to costing them a lot of money.

During the time that the property was on the market, they moved out for some weeks to allow painters to repaint. They later discovered that the painters had set up a meth lab in their house. Certainly that would indicate noxious energies, alien or otherwise.

They did not run into such 'bad luck' on their new property.

If you find that you cannot get a place clear of very detrimental alien energy, it may be wise to give up, because it is usually a sign of very powerful energy, and you may be at risk if you keep working to clear it. However, it is rare to find energy this terrible. Bear in mind that when you fail at what you are trying to do, sometimes it is the Universe's way of protecting you. Don't let ego cause you to persist when you feel something is dangerous or you aren't seeing results. We all run into situations we can't handle, and the best thing to do is to bow out gracefully.

Danger

On very rare occasions, if you tamper with an active experiment, stomping around within it so to speak, you can attract unwanted attention that could lead to an alien reaction that could be detrimental to you. This could be likened to trying to disempower a professional curse that is booby trapped. Your protection is therefore vital to your safety. Think of yourself as being stealthy and slipping into the lab and turning off the switch on the section of the experiment that affects just you, your property and loved ones. Do not attempt to shut an experiment down completely, as it is unlikely you can escape notice if you do that.

This type of clearing becomes more of a visualization than a stepwise clearing procedure, and each one is different. If you are tuned in intuitively, you can just follow what your inner guidance says to do after you have set your goals very clearly and specifically and done your protection. The visualization can take the form of you creeping into a lab late at night, looking for the switch that will turn off the part of the experiment affecting you and your property. Or you might look at it like a big electrical transformer and switching station or a telephone exchange or a bunch of computer servers. Whatever allows you to go in and turn off the part that is affecting you.

30

MINIMIZING ALIEN ENERGIES

In each of the three parts of this guide, the section on how to minimize the effects on you is priceless. Clearing energy of any kind follows a pattern, as you can see from this guide. Once you learn the pattern and the steps and master protection, you can clear most energies safely. However, the next level of mastery is to learn how to avoid being affected by such energies in the first place.

Think of how much it will save you to be bulletproof to these weird and sometimes dangerous forces. Spiritual seekers are often people who have opened themselves intuitively, and yet they haven't learned how to protect themselves from the often detrimental energies they come into contact with. One of the strange truths about being open to the possibility of these phenomena, and invisible energies in general, is that your intention to be 'open' can lead to unpleasant effects on you, because your system defines 'open' much more broadly than you think.

Very few people are naturally protected when they become more interested in spiritual or invisible things. Most people who have an interest in energies tend to be empathetic, which often equates to having weak energetic boundaries. The wounded healer is an example of an empathetic person who has opened herself to the possibility of helping others heal, but hasn't got strong boundaries and ends up accumulating all the nasty energies her clients dump during sessions. If you are going to explore energies and healing and personal transformation, you will benefit greatly from learning to minimize the ill effects of noxious energies on you.

To be less affected by alien energies and other noxious forms of energy, you need to do self-work. You are unique, so there is no single path we can point out to you.

The first thing you need to do is to think about your goals beyond your interest in healing or energy. What kind of health do you want to experience physically, mentally and emotionally? How comfortable do you want to feel? How powerful do you want to be? How do you want to exercise your free will and ability to manifest the life you want?

Getting clear on your goals is important before you ask to be guided as to what to do. This is a step most people skip. I'm not sure why, but so many New Age thinkers believe they should act like leaves on the water and just 'go with the flow'. If that is what you want out of life, to be carried somewhere without any input from you, that's fine. But if you want to create something particular with your life, then you need to have specific goals. You can go with the flow after you set your intentions.

One of your goals definitely needs to be that of being safe and staying healthy during your journey as you encounter and clear energies. You want to promote strong energetic boundaries and transform any beliefs or habits that weaken you.

Write your goals down in your journal. Revisit them periodically and refine them. You will find that they become more detailed and specific over time, and that as you do that, your guidance gets better. With respect to alien energies, your viewpoint on power and your attitude about free will are very important. Even advanced beings do not have the right to run your life. You have free will and the power to exercise it, even if they are technologically advanced.

Once you are clear on your goals, ask the Universe to show you the best method at this time for achieving your goals of staying strong and healthy when facing noxious energies. There are many wonderful healing and transformational methods. If you are a dowser, you can use dowsing to confirm which method is best for you. Otherwise, just choose whichever one draws you the most.

We have used many methods, but tapping and toning are two very good and effective methods. Tapping does rely on a certain level of verbal ability and self-reflection. Toning is very simple and requires only that you have a clear goal. Methods like Reiki and Spiritual Healing are not as focused for helping you with your goals, but are excellent for overall health. It is useful to have several healing or transformational methods in your toolbox.

With respect to alien energies, fear is your biggest weakness. Remove fear from your system as best you can. Another energy that will weaken you is powerlessness. Learn to accept your power, and you will be less at risk for alien energies to affect you.

Do self-work regularly. Several times a week is good. Write up the results in your journal. Do not expect to become bulletproof overnight. It took many years for you to get to where you are, so be patient if it takes a few years to get somewhere else. Overnight change is often not very comfortable, to say the least, so be grateful and be patient. Notice your feelings when you think about alien energies. Are you less fearful? Do you have confidence that you can live your life without the interference of aliens? Your emotions are a good way to gauge your progress.

31

SUMMARY

Some aliens and their energies are detrimental to humans. The effects of alien energies can be confused with any other type of noxious energy, so dowsing is the best way to determine if alien energies are the problem. It is possible to transform and clear alien energies using a simple stepwise method in most cases, but there are rare occurrences that require other techniques, or even that are advisable to walk away from. Dowsing is the best method to identify those situations and how to deal with them.

Always approach the concept of aliens with caution and respect. Fear is counterproductive, and we recommend self-work to help you realize that even scary things like tarantulas, snakes and aliens have their place in the Universe, and that you can live in peace and harmony with them. You have free will and the right to choose not to be harmed, and by doing regular self-work, you can minimize the chances that you will encounter unpleasant alien energies.

HOW DOWSING CAN HELP

The power of dowsing is that you can use it to answer any question your mind can't answer. So when you want to know more about what is causing your symptoms, dowsing is a perfect technique to use, either to identify energies and their effects or to pick the best method to clear them.

This guide is not a dowsing course. We have another guide on developing your intuition and a course in a book mentioned in the Resources section.

Learning to dowse is very straightforward, but like any skill, dowsing has complexities, and you will get better results if you get good training. What follows is just a taste of what is involved in dowsing, so you can decide if you want to plunge in and learn how to do it. Without dowsing, you won't be able to get much detail when working on ghosts, curses and aliens. We strongly urge you to learn how to dowse.

Dowsing involves several steps:

1. Be clear about your goal
2. Form a good question that is very detailed and specific and has a yes or no answer

3. Focus on the question and empty your mind (this is called getting into a dowsing state)
4. Be curious but not attached as to what the answer is
5. Receive the answer

Steps 1-4 seem pretty easy to understand, though I must warn you that each one involves work and practice to master. Make a mistake at any step, and your answer will probably be incorrect.

Step 5, the actual answer, is just a small part of the process, but it may be the part which is most unfamiliar to you. When you dowse, you can either use a tool like a pendulum, or you can dowse without a tool, using some part of your body to give you the answer (the latter is what kinesiologists do).

There are many methods of deviceless dowsing, but one of the most common and most reliable is the Body Sway. The Body Sway uses the forward or backward motion of your body to indicate 'yes' or 'no.'

Give it a try. Stand straight, relaxed, feet shoulder width apart. Close your eyes. Breathe normally. Think of the city or country you were born in. Ask, "Was I born in _____?" (Fill in the blank with the correct answer.) Wait in a curious and detached way to see what your body does. Forward is usually 'yes.' Did you get forward motion?

Don't be upset if you did not. Maybe your 'yes' is backward motion. Check out your 'no' answer by doing it again, but this time, insert an answer you know is wrong for your birthplace. As long as you get a different motion for 'yes' and 'no,' you can dowse and get an answer.

How accurate your answer will be depends on how good and clear your question is, how detached yet focused you are and a number of other factors we won't go into here, but are covered in our dowsing course.

The purpose of this demonstration was to show you that it is possible to tap into your intuition in a focused way and get an answer to a question right now. We used your birthplace, because it's easy, and you know what is right and wrong. When you actually dowse in the real world, you won't know if your answer is right or wrong, which is why we urge you to take our course, because it goes into detail about proper technique.

Scales are used in dowsing to go beyond yes/no answers and find out the level of intensity of a noxious energy. There are many kinds of scales, but 0-10 and +10 to -10 are most common. Finding out a number value consists of asking what the intensity is and either saying each number until you get 'yes,' using a chart that shows the numbers, or just thinking the numbers in your head and going through them as a list until you get a 'yes.'

FINAL SUMMARY

If you have read this entire guide and tried to put into practice what we are teaching, you will notice that there are many similarities when dealing with these three very different types of conscious energies. That is because energy clearing in general follows certain patterns. You must have a clear goal. You need adequate protection. You need a method for focusing your intention and transforming or clearing the detrimental energies.

In all cases, detrimental energy effects in your life can be minimized by working on yourself to vibrate with power, harmony and non-judgment. In fact, all types of energy clearing and healing follow this pattern. Change yourself, and you change the world. Work on your own energies to become safer, healthier and happier.

We encourage you to focus more time and effort on what you intend to create—safety, joy and good health—rather than on what you think is 'wrong' or causing you harm. While learning to identify and clear noxious energies is a step toward conscious living and greater health, if you focus too much on finding 'wrong' things and fixing them, you will keep creating them. By putting more time into harmonizing your life, you show your intention and expectation that you can create harmony.

Besides, you don't need to fix everything that's wrong in your life to experience happiness and well-being. It is surprisingly hard to make this shift in focus, but it will give you faster progress. It turns your focus inward and makes it like a laser.

Dowsing is the most powerful tool we have in our very full toolkit. It expands your ability to know what to do and to be safe while doing it. We hope you are interested in learning this natural skill.

HOW NOT TO BE OVERWHELMED

We created *The Busy Person's Guides* to help people like you who have a lot on their plates. We know how overwhelming modern life can be at times, and we want to help you simplify things and reduce stress. Stress is a major cause of ill health. We'd like to help you reduce stress in your life, so you can be productively busy without being overwhelmed, so we've added this bonus section with tips that have proven useful for us. We're sharing these because we've applied them and seen good results in our lives.

Do Not Multitask

You may think that if you are able to do more than one thing at a time, you will be more effective in your life. This is not the case. Focus on doing one thing at a time and doing it well. Being able to focus on just one thing is vital for learning how to clear energy, so it is excellent practice.

Slow Down

We fall into the habit of feeling if we are moving fast, we are getting more done. That is not the case. Slow down and take your time. Instead of telling yourself how little time you have, tell yourself that you have all the time you need to get everything that needs doing done. Even if you do not believe this at first, do it. Your perception controls your reality. If you feel you don't have enough time, you probably won't have enough time. Sounds strange, but it works.

Be Sure To Have Goals

Don't have tasks, have goals. It is a never-ending and stressful life if you just keep lists of tasks you have to do. The lists never end, and the stress builds. Instead, have specific goals. Tasks should be done with intention, as in doing something because you believe it will help you achieve your goal. If you find you are doing things to please others or that the tasks are mindless and don't help you achieve a goal, find a way to stop doing them.

Accept Help

Don't cling to the belief that you must do everything alone, that no one else is as competent as you, or that no one cares to support you. These beliefs lead to stress. There is always help. **Don't make excuses to turn help down.** Train yourself to accept help.

Expect Positive Outcomes

Cultivate the attitude that whatever happens is going to give you an overall positive outcome. Maybe it is not the result you wanted. Perhaps it happened to teach you something you need to know or to help you see something you need to change, without which you would never reach your goal. If you find the opportunity in every event, even the unpleasant ones, you will become a happier and less stressed person. And you will be more empowered.

Avoid Measuring Your Value By How Busy You Are

We have mostly been raised to value work and to feel we are better people if we are more productive. We tend to measure our worth by how much work we do, or by the quality of that work. But we have found that happiness comes from doing what you love and that blurring the boundary between work and play is a positive thing. We no longer have to justify to people how busy we are to show we are worthy.

People are going to judge you no matter what you do. What matters is what you think of yourself. You are worthy regardless of how you spend your time. You have inherent value as a human being. Don't trap yourself in the belief that busy is better. Busy is just busy. If it makes you happy, fine.

Eat, Drink & Exercise Appropriately

Eat real, organic food, not processed junk. Drink lots of pure water, not tap water, beer or soda. Get enough sleep and exercise your body, especially by getting out in Nature regularly. Taking care of yourself is a sign of good self-esteem. Putting yourself last or making excuses about mistreating your body is a sign of low self-respect and sometimes even a sign of subconsciously hating the physical realm and being on earth. Self-love is a positive thing. Take care of yourself, and you will be more able to take care of those you love and to be happy in human form.

Practice A Method For Self-Growth

Meditate, do tapping or self-hypnosis or a healing technique that helps you to change and grow. Invest in yourself. Look forward to becoming a more authentic, happy person.

THESE SUGGESTIONS MAY SOUND silly or self-evident or even woo-woo, but if you take them to heart, we believe that you will see positive changes in your life. Ultimately, the goal of not being stressed and too busy is a very good goal to have. We want to help you enjoy an empowered, happy life.

RESOURCES

You can find many resources online about energy clearing and dowsing. We have a dowsing course in a book entitled *Learn Dowsing: Your Natural Psychic Power*. We have authored over 20 books on dowsing and related topics. Visit your favorite online retailer for a complete list. Our Amazon author pages are a good resource for that purpose.

If you can find a local dowsing chapter, you will enjoy spending time with like-minded people and expand your dowsing horizons. There are also metaphysical conferences and events in person and online that will help you learn more about both energy clearing and dowsing. These events are changing rapidly with the changing environment, so we won't list specific ones, because so many have disappeared in recent years. But a good online search will show you what is available in your area and online.

Keep learning. Find your tribe and have fun!

PLEASE LEAVE A REVIEW

We created this series for busy people who want to learn effective and safe energy clearing techniques to improve their lives. If you enjoyed *The Busy Person's Guides* and think others would, too, please leave a review where you purchased this book to help future readers. Thanks.

ABOUT THE AUTHORS

Maggie and Nigel Percy met online in 2000 through their mutual love of dowsing. They spent the next 20+ years serving a global clientele with dowsing and energy clearing methods. During that time, they presented at many conferences, created the online Dowsing World Summit and gave free dowsing training through videos and articles on their websites. They've written over 20 books on dowsing and metaphysical topics and have published fiction using the pen names Maggie McPhee and Andrew Elgin. To see all their books, visit your favorite online retailer.

www.ingramcontent.com/pod-product-compliance
Lightning Source LLC
Chambersburg PA
CBHW070720160426
43192CB00009B/1261